Beginning Interpretative Inquiry

Beginning   ... he use of 'inquiry'
rather than   ... ouse explores how
inquiry is a   ...g of both research
and evaluat   ...ations that many
academics a   ...nic disciplines are
successfully   ...e enterprises share
much in co   ...ts; some that are
primarily re   ...hat effectively and
seamlessly c

Having p   ... of interpretative
inquiry, the   ...explores all stages
of the proce

- how th
- underst
- how to
- data co
- effectiv
- writing

Complete w   ...is vital new book
is an essentia   ...em plan, conduct
and evaluate   ...approaches.

Richard E.   ...ersity, Wisconsin,
USA and a   ...yndŵr University
Wrexham, Wales, UK.

Beginning Interpretative Inquiry

A step-by-step approach to
research and evaluation

Richard E. Morehouse

Routledge
Taylor & Francis Group

LONDON AND NEW YORK

First published 2012
by Routledge
2 Park Square, Milton Park, Abingdon, Oxon OX14 4RN

Simultaneously published in the USA and Canada
by Routledge
711 Third Avenue, New York, NY 10017

Routledge is an imprint of the Taylor & Francis Group, an informa business

© 2012 Richard E. Morehouse

British Library Cataloguing in Publication Data
A catalogue record for this book is available from the British Library

Library of Congress Cataloging-in-Publication Data
Morehouse, Richard.
Beginning Interpretative Inquiry : a step-by-step approach to research and
evaluation / Richard Morehouse. -- 1st ed.
p. cm.
1. Education--Research--Methodology. 2. Qualitative research. 3. Quantitative
research. I. Title.
LB1028.M6437 2011
370.72--dc22
2011005290

ISBN: 978-0-415-60188-7 (hbk)
ISBN: 978-0-415-60189-4 (pbk)
ISBN: 978-0-203-81824-4 (ebk)

Typeset in Galliard by
Saxon Graphics Ltd, Derby

MIX
Paper from
responsible sources
FSC
www.fsc.org   FSC® C004839

Printed and bound in Great Britain by
TJ International Ltd, Padstow, Cornwall

Contents

List of figures

List of tables

List of research exercises

Acknowledgements

It is not possible to acknowledge all the people that have aided me in this project. I must begin with the recognition of my colleague Pamela Maykut with whom I wrote our first book, *Beginning Qualitative Research* (1994). That first book was the basis for much of my experience as a researcher that followed. As I began to think anew about this project the work of Michael Westerman of New York University and Steven Yanchar of the Brigham Young University were of great help in rethinking my perspective on mixed methods research (interpretative inquiry). Both men provided assistance with email correspondence and their published work was invaluable in shaping my own thinking. Dr. Mary T. Sheerin, my mentor during my doctoral studies, read the first chapters of this work. Dr. Susan T. Gardner, Professor of Philosophy at Capilano University in Vancouver, also read the first chapters. Their comments and suggestions were very valuable. Patrick Costello of Glyndŵr University, Wrexham, read most of the manuscript. His insight and support were invaluable. Philip Basset, Head of the School of Education and Community, Glyndŵr University, Wrexham, provided the opportunity for my appointment as Visiting Professor at the School of Education and Community, Glyndŵr University, Wrexham. As I was sorting out some of the ideas for this book, the engagement of the faculty and students at Glyndŵr University provided a stimulating and provocative environment for reflection.

Valerie Kokott-Rebhahn as co-instructor in several research classes contributed to some of the projects discussed in this work and generally to my understanding of research and how to explain what research is about. The entire Psychology Department at Viterbo University also needs to be recognized for their support and good humor. The students in those research classes also help to shape my understanding of many ideas that I thought I knew until I attempted to explain them. A special thanks to my fellow researchers, a band of students whose excitement about research fueled my own excitement. The students and I formed an ad hoc research group. We called it PERT. All errors and omissions, of course, are mine.

The folks at Routledge also need to be thanked for their patience and understanding. (I am especially appreciative of the copy editor.) I would like to single out Anna Clarkson, Ivor Goodson, and Philip Mudd.

A special thanks to Rita Morehouse for her support and good humor over more than 40 years and especially during the last weeks of this project, when, with better planning, we could have been enjoying more of the sun in south Texas.

Chapter 1

Introduction

This introduction provides a short answer to the question "What is interpretative inquiry?" (A more elaborate answer will be provided in Chapter 2.) After addressing the "what" question, I will briefly address the "why" question: specifically, is a book on interpretative research needed? I will also address some of the criticisms and barriers to research in the interpretative tradition and provide some preliminary answers to the critics. The final section of the introduction presents the plan for the rest of the book.

What is interpretative research?

Interpretative research is research within the hermeneutic and phenomenological traditions. The dictionary (Apple Dictionary, Version 2.0.2) says that hermeneutics serve to interpret or explain. That seems to be too much of a circular definition, that is, interpretative research is interpretative. Stated more clearly, hermeneutic research is interpretation within the specific framework of whole-part relationships; that is, one begins with the big picture, the Gestalt or whole, and then looks at the individual pieces in order to better understand the whole which leads back to a new look at the pieces, in an increasing spiral of complexity and relational connectivity. It is in this manner that an understanding of a phenomenon is acquired. Phenomenology is defined as an effort to understand experience as lived. "It is looking for what it is as a fact for us, before any thematizing" (Merleau-Ponty 1962: xv). As an approach to research, phenomenological inquiry examines conscious experiences of individuals as well as their direct experience of the world and their interaction in the world. A phenomenological perspective also sees experiences as embodied, embedded in the world (the lived-experience) and as complex and inter-connective. The hermeneutic/phonological perspective privileges human agency, lived experience, practice, and interpretation in context (Yanchar 2006). It also locates the inquirer in the world, the same world as the phenomenon under scrutiny. In other words, interpretative research has a worldview that differs from a positivist's perspective that has an impartial or "God's" eye view of the world that separates the observer from the world and also sees the world as more or less static.

As all research is to examine something or some relationship, why, one might ask, not conduct standard experimental research? What one wishes to avoid by doing interpretative inquiry is reductionism. Reductionism is the practice of analyzing and describing a complex phenomenon, especially a mental or social phenomenon, by looking at the simplest representations of the phenomena. These representations are held to be at a deeper and more fundamental level. "By focusing on what is usually a small number of causal factors, it renders a complex domain cognitively trackable" (Trout 2008). This becomes problematic when these reductions are said to provide a sufficient explanation. An alternative definition of explanation is a reason or justification given for an action or belief (Apple Dictionary, Version 2.0.2). Reasons and justifications come from an understanding of human interaction. Reason and justifications usually refer to agents and relationships. It is conscious and responsible actions of an agent that are explained via reasons and justifications from a hermeneutic/phenomenological perspective.

Traditional experimental research is generally thought to lean toward reductionist explanations as they oversimplify complex human relationships and are more-or-less static. This orientation to research is widely used in psychology and education and is often thought to be synonymous with research. In fact some in the educational research and policy community take the definition of research as proof that this is the only kind of legitimate research so seriously that they wish to exclude all research that is not experimental and proof-oriented (Moya 1990: 67).

I will now explore the kinds of research included within the interpretative inquiry framework before going on to examining more fully the controversy surrounding what counts as research. Research that explains and interprets is of three kinds: qualitative, quantitative, and mixed (qualitative and quantitative). Most, but not all qualitative inquiry is within the interpretative perspective. Some, but not all, quantitative and mixed quantitative or qualitative inquiry fit into the model of positivist research. Yanchar and Williams (2006) specifically reject the rigid two-paradigm position looking instead for criteria that would allow two modes of inquiry to be used together if they are found to be compatible. In what is to follow, the interpretative model will be wholly embraced, and an argument will made that the interpretative model can accommodate both qualitative and quantitative inquiry.

An interpretative perspective views the world and the observer as situated in a practice or activity within a lived world. That lived world is always *in medias res*, or in the middle of things; it is a view that places an agent in a living culture (Westerman 2006). A specific example of research that is conducted from an interpretative perspective is Ann L. Brown's project called Community of Thinking and Learning (1997). In this project, Brown explains the emergence over time of strategic and metacognitive knowledge in children between the ages of 6 and 12 years of age and the complex social and interpersonal environment that surrounds those changes. Bruner writes about this project in *The Culture of Education* (1996) arguing that understanding complex relational encounters such as teaching and learning come about by looking to how individuals act, reflect, and collaborate within a given cultural setting.

To determine what to include as interpretative inquiry, I need to ask several questions. The first question to ask is, what is to be interpreted? The answer is human action, human practice. This perspective begins with an understanding of how one studies human beings. Jerome Bruner in *Acts of Meaning* (1990) writes that the proper study of humans looks to action as opposed to behavior, meaning rather than information, and agents instead of subjects. An inquiry project that seeks to understand the connections between teachers and students as they engage in learning new skills and applying new knowledge fits Bruner's perspective for understanding humans as agents. Interpretative research, I would argue, is the research that seeks to take these three orientations (agency, action, and meaning) as the framework for research in education and psychology. Bruner goes on to explore how a psychology that is immersed in culture can be studied. As culture is essential to understanding human agency, our inquiry project must be organized around those meanings. It is the public and shared nature of culture that provides the vehicle within which inquiry is conducted. Interpretative inquiry explores shared meaning and shared concepts as well as shared modes of discourse for negotiating differences in meaning and interpretation (Bruner 1990: 12–13).

In a similar vein to Bruner's statement, Steven Yanchar (2006), arguing for a hermeneutic perspective, privileges human agency, lived experience, practice, and interpretation in context. This orientation to or perspective on research focuses on negotiation and interpretation.

The second question is, how is the action or relationship to be inquired into? The short answer is by looking at the phenomenon as a process rather than as a thing. Carlos Moya, in *The Philosophy of Action* (2003), argues that placing action and agents within a context in motion is essential if one does not wish to destroy the very ideas of action and agency.

> Moreover, the idea of agency conflicts with our understanding causally related events where no room can be found for agents, for being capable of initiating new causal chains. The problem is that even the smallest gap in this causal network would mean its complete collapse.
>
> (Moya 2003: 9)

In further support for the study of action, Michael Westerman states that as "a person is always already involved in meaningful practical activities in the world, and not a spectator fundamentally separated from the world" (2006: 196). Therefore, the researcher is obliged to look at the person as an agent in context acting in and with others in the world.

The third question to ask is what is the relationship of the researcher to issues of values? The study of human action is an implicit study of the values that direct action and to be blind to those values is to inevitably misinterpret action. Robert Selman's research as documented in *The Promotion of Social Awareness: Powerful Lessons from the Partnership between Developmental Theory and Classroom Practice* (2003) shows his commitment to values.

> I belong to a group of practitioners and researchers concerned with the promotion of social competence and the prevention of the problems associated with impaired social development – primarily in children and youth, but also in adults. We believe that these objectives are important not only in the lives of individuals but also in our society's ability to provide – or fail to provide – for the good of all its members. In particular we are interested in research and practice that help build social competencies in children and youth who are growing up under difficult circumstances – that is, those who face psycho-pathology in their families, poverty in their neighborhoods, or prejudice in the wider culture in which they must make their way.
>
> (Selman 2003: 2)

To conclude this section, interpretative inquiry is defined by agency, action, and the interpretation of meaning within complex relationships and values based. Interpretative inquiry "sees the meanings we live by as permeating and shaping the practice and institutions of others and the world 'out there' much as they belong to our 'inner' life'" (Bishop 2007: 71). This orientation to inquiry is also oriented toward understanding process over product. Finally, interpretative inquiry is values oriented. "The way we experience everyday life, values, and meaning are both in us and in the world around us" (ibid.). All three of these orientations are a form of practice.

Interpretative inquiry is a hermeneutic/phenomenological enterprise that may include qualitative, quantitative, and mixed data as long as the interpretation is contextual, creative, conceptually aware, coherent, and critically reflective (with apologies to Yanchar and Williams (2006) for what I hope is a minor modification of their thesis on methods usage). In other words, if quantitative and qualitative inquiry are to be used in the same study, they should interact with each other in a manner that is informed by seeing the part in terms of the whole and the whole with reference to each of its parts in an ongoing interplay that increases understanding. The inquirer, in other words, must be aware that the use of quantitative methods doesn't nudge her toward a positivist orientation. Moya (1990: 9) warns us "that every attempt to account for action within this deterministic picture, that is, every attempt to consider action as nodes of causal networks, will destroy what is specific about agency."

Why a book on interpretative research?

There are already many books on qualitative, quantitative, and mixed methods. There are no books to my knowledge that accomplish the two things that this work hopes to do:

1   take students, beginning researchers, or anyone else who has not conducted a research project that uses both qualitative and quantitative data and approaches to gathering data, and
2   provide the underlying philosophical support and explanation that allows the beginning researchers to both complete their project and to defend the moves and strategies they used in conducting their research and presenting their findings, with an emphasis on the need for embracing an interpretative orientation when studying human action.

Let's start with the second point – the philosophical underpinnings. Is it important to know the underlying philosophy that guides research? Isn't it enough to know how to conduct a research project? I would argue that it is important, if not essential, to know the philosophical underpinnings of what you are doing as a researcher as it aids the development within the inquirer of several important qualities. Specifically, it enhances the ability to notice potential research problems as they arise, the ability to defend your work to supporters and critics, and the confidence to ask good research questions and match the questions with appropriate data collection methods and data analysis procedures. Understanding the philosophical underpinnings of a research project or evaluation provides a foundation on which to select data-gathering strategies, frame research questions, include and exclude various methods of data analysis, and to make a case for many other research choices that are required as the project moves from one phase to the next. Pardon a small aside here that will be developed later, in Chapter 9. One of the weaknesses that I have noted in some published qualitative studies is a less than comprehensive method discussion. A comprehensive and thorough method section is even more important in studies that use mixed methods. Research methods are at the heart of any research project and without a solid philosophical understanding of how methods and data analysis support each other; it is difficult to make a coherent case for your choices. Yanchar and Williams (2006) present five guidelines for method use. In their article, coherence is one of the guidelines. While cautioning against inflexibility with regard to methods usage, they state that coherence "would entail a recognition that questions, methods, practices, and interpretations should fit strategically within some larger theoretical purpose and do so without giving way to uninterruptable contradictions or self-refutation" (Yanchar and Williams 2006: 9).

Now to the first justification for this book – the need for a book that takes beginning researchers from the conception of the project or inquiry to the writing of the results. Inquiry (research and evaluation) is a process. Granted it is not necessarily a strictly linear process but it is a process nonetheless. This book is conceptualized as a process that develops or unfolds. You as a reader of this book will also be engaged in a process. Each chapter will have one or more inquiry exercises. These exercises are integral to a fuller understanding of the processes and products of an interpretative inquirer. My intention is to make them engaging and helpful as you learn step-by-step. Complete each exercise as you read unless otherwise directed.

Research exercise 1.1: Inquirer's notebook

As an aid to understanding the unfolding nature of your experiences as an inquirer, you are asked to start an inquirer's journal. This journal will be used for all the exercises undertaken as you read though the book. While you may use your laptop computer as your notebook, I suggest that you use a paper-bound notebook (your choice as to style, but pick something that is easy to carry with you and that may be accessed quickly and on the run). Your first assignment is to write your thoughts, fears, anticipations, and concerns as you begin your involvement as an interpretative inquirer. Your notes may be bullet points, sentence fragments, or complete sentences or paragraphs – the point is to begin your experiences as an interpretative inquirer.

Each step in the process is in a more-or-less sequential order. With the entry in your notebook, you have completed one of the first steps toward becoming an interpretative inquirer. I hope to lead undergraduate students, graduate students, and others as they work their way through a research or evaluation project. The book is designed so that as the beginning researchers complete one part of their project, the tools and information are available for them to tackle the next phase of their project.

My sense is that beginning inquirers not only need to know what they are currently doing, but what they will do next, and how each step in the process fits with the one that came before and the one that follows. Beginning inquirers need to be able to look in both directions from where they stand at the current moment in their project. In a surprising way, the ability to position themselves between what they have done and what they are about to do provides the inquirer with a certain flexibility in that it allows for recognizing and possibly correcting the inevitable missteps and mistakes that occur in all research and evaluation projects. By supplying a complete beginning through end arch, people new to research gain the confidence and perspective that is required to complete a research or evaluation project.

How the book unfolds

This work is divided into two sections: Part I is "A philosophical foundation for interpretative inquiry". Part II is "From ideas to publication."

The first section has three chapters. An overview of the philosophical underpinnings of research is the opening chapter. Chapter 2 entitled "Before beginning your inquiry project," extends the argument presented here regarding the nature of interpretative inquiry. I begin by distinguishing interpretative, hermeneutic perspectives from more positivism orientations and go on to discuss qualitative, quantitative, and mixed approaches to inquiry from a philosophical perspective while laying the groundwork for the practical implications that will follow. This chapter makes the case for why a philosophical perspective is helpful. Chapter3, "The interpretative stance: Inquiry *in medias res*," explores the implications of agency, action, and meaning within a context of both the researcher and the focus of inquiry being "in the middle of things." A final short chapter ends the first section. This chapter (Chapter 4) is "A closer look at what counts as interpretative inquiry." The premise that informs these closing remarks is that while it is important to define one's topic positively it is also helpful to look closely at what the topic is not. By looking especially at examples of inquiry that almost fit into the interpretative orientation, a sharper distinction can be made and, I hope, a clearer picture for the beginning interpretative inquirer can be made of what they expect to face as they begin their projects.

The second section of the book "From ideas to publication" provides a step-by-step approach to conducting a research or evaluation project. Chapter 5 lays out what will be presented in each of the chapters by providing some key terms and their definitions. I then show how these key terms are related to each other and how the processes of interpretative inquiry fit together as elements of a research or evaluation project. This process is, in fact, how one designs a project. Chapter 6 addresses the question: Where do inquiry ideas come from? Those new to inquiry often have many questions worth exploring as a research or an evaluation topic. What new inquirers lack is a sense of how to move from vague questions to a focused research question. This chapter helps the new researcher make those moves. It also aids the new researcher in figuring out the nature of the data they are seeking, that is, does their question require quantitative information, qualitative information, or a combination of both types of information. I next look at our inquiry sample (Chapter 7). The chapter begins the work of writing the proposal for the research or evaluation project. It includes the search of the literature as well as the preparing of the review of the literature. Discussion of the writing of the problem statement, the design of the project and the inquiry sample are developed in this chapter. Chapter 8 examines data collection mechanisms and data analysis. In addition to looking at the similarities and differences of qualitative and quantitative data collection and analysis, I will specifically address the types of data and the approaches to data collection that fit with my understanding of an interpretative inquiry, that is one that focuses on actions, meaning, and agents *in medias res*. Chapter 9 discusses the ethics of research including the role of the Institutional Review Board and its relation to launching the research project. Chapter 10 is writing for publication. The chapter on writing the results I have chosen to frame in terms of writing for publication rather than merely writing up the results. The reason for this is my firm belief that inquiry should see the light of day to be criticized and utilized, and also that new researchers should aim for publication. It is not our belief that everything is worth publishing but that new researchers should not prejudge their own work before it is completed. Therefore, they should aim initially for publication and only pull back from that idea if the final product is such that it will not contribute to the larger body of knowledge.

Several appendixes end the book. These appendixes are intended to provide a specific example of work that has been conducted in conjunction with graduate or undergraduate students. Some of these projects were class projects and some of the projects were conducted as ad hoc research teams constructed through casual conversations with students interested in research. Along with the example, I have provided a brief introduction and conclusion to situate the example in context.

Part 1

A philosophical foundation for interpretative inquiry

Chapter 2

Before beginning your inquiry project

For over 15 years there has been considerable discussion about the relationship between qualitative and quantitative research and evaluation. This discussion has sometimes taken the perspective that there are two irreconcilable paradigms: Naturalist and Positivist (Lincoln and Guba 1985). While those debates still go on (Bredo 2009; Guba 1990; Halling and Lawrence 1999; Held 1998; Howe 2009; Johnson 2009; Tillman 2009), there has been much new written about how to think through the two paradigm arguments.

Table 2.1 illustrates the differences in the worldview of the naturalist and the positivist paradigms.

Table 2.1 Why the two paradigms are incompatible.

	Positivist position	*Naturalist position*
On the nature of reality	Human beings construct reality by interpreting their perceptions of it.	Reality is independent of the human observer.
On how knowledge is found	We construct our realities from our tacit understanding and tangible experience.	Admissible evidence is observable and tangible.
On the relationship between the inquirer and the inquired	The inquirer and what is to be inquired into interact to influence the outcome of the inquiry.	An inquiry can be conducted with minimal influence on the subject of the investigation.
On the role values play in research	Values are an inherent quality of human inquiry.	Values play little or no role in understanding the world.
On causal links	There are complex interactions and multidirectional influences between and among human beings that preclude linear cause-effect relationships.	Carefully designed projects can lead to lawful and predictable relationships in the human and natural world.
On inquiry in the social sciences	Meaningful and in-depth understanding is the aim of social science.	Social sciences aims to predict and control events. These predictions are transferable to similar situations

Source: modified from Maykut and Morehouse 1994: 12.

My position is that the differences between the two paradigms make it impossible to do research or evaluation by taking parts of each worldview as a part of one's approach to inquiry. It was the incompatibility of these two worldviews that led me to take sides in the paradigm debate.

In *Beginning Qualitative Research* (Maykut and Morehouse 1994), I supported the non-compatible paradigm position as this position was seen as helpful to researchers new to qualitative inquiry and as my co-author and I saw this position as helping to establish a mindset for framing research questions in a qualitative manner and conducting qualitative studies. I further thought that the experimental mindset was dominant enough to unwittingly shape research questions and practices even as those new to qualitative inquiry worked to initiate their projects. Over the past 15 years qualitative inquiry has become more widely accepted. Stephen Yanchar (Yanchar and Williams 2006; Yanchar 2006) and Michael Westerman (2005, 2006) are among several of the thinkers that influenced my understanding of the subject. Reading these researchers pulled me away from the two-paradigm position. I will explain shortly, the two-paradigm position no longer makes sense to me as a researcher.

This chapter is intended to provide the information needed to create a mindset for conducting interpretative inquiry, that is research and evaluation projects that are grounded in action, meaning, and agency. The chapter begins by situating philosophical questions within a research context. After fully embedding research within a set of philosophical questions, I then examine the two research paradigms more fully. This section also documents my struggle with the two research paradigms. I then move beyond the two paradigm models arguing that most research in the human sciences is conducted within the naturalist framework. From the naturalist side of the divide, I look at an interpretative orientation to research, first defining it and then making a case for the importance of it.

How does philosophy fit into our understanding of research issues? First, how does philosophy fit into a discussion of research? A quote from *Women's Ways of Knowing: The Development of Voice, Self, and Mind* (Belenky *et al.* 1986) provides insight into how philosophy matters in everyday life as well as in research. In the opening paragraph of *Women's Ways of Knowing*, they write:

> We do not think of the ordinary person as preoccupied with such difficult and profound questions as: What is truth? What is authority? To whom do I listen? What counts as evidence? How do I know what I know? Yet to ask ourselves these questions and reflect on our answers is more than an intellectual exercise, for our basic assumptions about the nature of truth and reality and the origins of knowledge shape the way we see the world and ourselves as participants in it. They affect our definitions of ourselves, our sense of control over life events, our views of teaching and learning, and our conceptions of morality
> (Belenky *et al.* 1986: 3)

The rest of *Women's Ways of Knowing* illustrates how the answers to the above questions affect one's voice, self, and mind. In many ways the philosophical questions asked by Mary Belenky and her colleagues are the same philosophical questions that we as scholarly inquirers must ask and answer if we are going to have our figurative feet firmly planted on solid philosophical ground.

Using these questions as a backdrop, let us explore the issues with a somewhat more direct look at scholarly inquiry. What is it that scholars involved in inquiry do? They ask questions that can be answered by gathering and analyzing data. This is a practitioner's definition of empirical study. A more scholarly definition of an empirical study is one that is based on, concerned with, or verifiable by observation or experience rather than theory or pure logic. Having defined empirical inquiry, let's look at the nature of the philosophical questions that need to be asked and answered. Philosophers divide the questions asked above by Mary Belenky and colleagues (1986) into five categories: ontological, epistemological, logical, teleological, and ethical. The authors of *Women's Ways of Knowing* first ask: What is truth? This question is a question about both the nature of reality (ontology) and about how we understand or know about that reality (epistemology). The next set of questions: What is authority? To whom do I listen? What counts as evidence? And how do I know what I know? are questions of epistemology and to some extent teleology, that is, they address questions about the relationship between the knower and the known (epistemology) as well as the purpose of learning or knowing (teleology). We agree with the authors of *Women's Ways of Knowing* that these questions shape our way of seeing the world, and we would add that they also shape our understanding of how to conduct research. Questions of logic are not as easily seen in the cited quote. However, what counts as evidence, or more specifically, what conclusions may be drawn from the evidence is a question of logic. Ethics is also an important element of research. We agree that the way we answer all the above questions influences our sense of morality, or our ethics. Ethics is important to scholarly inquiry on many different levels. We will address many of the ethical issues of scholarly inquiry.

Table 2.2 presents the philosophical questions and connects them directly to scholarly inquiry. These questions and our answers to them will guide much of our thinking in this chapter. Moreover, asking and answering these philosophical questions will influence our choice of methods of data collection and analysis. With some background in the philosophical underpinnings of research you will be better able to understand what you are doing, explain the choices you make as scholarly inquirers and be provided with a basis for grounding your answers to questions from critics and supporters regarding how you conducted your inquiry projects. It is to the extent that philosophy guides us in addressing these issues that philosophy becomes practical.

Table 2.2 Framing research within a philosophical perspective.

Areas of philosophy as they relate to research	Questions
1. Ontology raises questions about the nature of reality.	What is the nature of the world? What is real? What counts as evidence?
2. Epistemology is interested in the origins and nature of knowing and the construction of knowledge.	What is the relationship between the knower and the known? What role do values play in understanding?
3. Logic, as it relates to research, deals with principles of demonstration and verification.	Are causal links between bits of information possible?
4. Teleology is generally concerned with questions of purpose.	What is research for?
5. Ethics is the branch of knowledge that deals with moral principles.	What is my responsibility to the subjects and the people I am studying?

Source: modified from Maykut and Morehouse 1994: 4

Take a minute or two to reflect on these basic philosophical questions. Mary Belenky and her colleagues (1986) made the case for the importance of addressing philosophical questions. Following the lead of these authors you are invited to work through the research exercise below. Also refer to Table 2.2 as you engage with this research exercise.

Research exercise 2.1: Exploring the role of philosophy as a research tool

Read these two articles.

Courtland, M. C. and Leslie, L. (2010) Beliefs and practices of three literacy instructors in elementary teacher education, *The Alberta Journal of Educational Research*, 56(1): 19–30.

Ireson, J. and Hallam, S. (2009) Academic self-concepts in adolescents: Relations with achievement and ability groupings, *Learning and Instruction*, 19(3): 201–213.

After reading each of these research articles see which article fits better with the naturalist paradigm and which fits best with the positivist paradigm. Do you find a difference in the way the authors seem to have answered the basic philosophical questions in Table 2.2? Describe the difference in a short essay.

This exercise is designed to help you understand some of the differences between the two paradigms. I do not claim that qualitative and naturalistic are synonymous, nor that quantitative and positivist are the same. This exercise is intended to provide an early example of qualitative and quantitative research. Later in the chapter the case will be made that most research leans toward the naturalist side of the continuum.

What is the nature of the philosophical debate regarding research paradigms?

One of the major debates within the research community is about the two paradigms and mixed methods studies. This debate focuses on how one's worldview affects conducting research. Another debate within the research community has to do with the selection of a model, the other definition of paradigm, for doing research. There are many models for doing research on the naturalistic side of the equation. These models for scholarly inquiry will be discussed later in this chapter.

The rise of the quantitative (positivist) viewpoint

In order to gain a better perspective on how an interpretative project might approach research and evaluation, it is helpful to briefly review the modern history of inquiry. This history arguably begins with John Locke and his *Essay on the Limits of Human Understanding* (1690). Often considered the first empiricist, he held that all knowledge is derived from sense-experience. This approach to understanding the world and other humans was applied to psychology and research methods by the behaviorists, most notably John Watson (1913) in his behaviorist manifesto, "Psychology as the behaviorist views it." B. F. Skinner, in many ways, epitomized that orientation to research in *Beyond Freedom and Dignity* (1971) and *About Behaviorism* (1974). Their approach to research saw humans as objects to be manipulated and controlled; researchers in this tradition called these human beings subjects.

Another long tradition that has affected the way we view inquiry in psychology, the human sciences, and education began with René Descartes. Descartes split mind and body into distinct parts; the body from his philosophical perspective was in a totally physical realm while the mind was in a totally mental one. The body was subject to the laws of nature and the mind was separate and subject to mental laws – ideally the laws of logic and reason. Descartes' philosophy led to introspection as a means of understanding human psychology (cf. Titchener 1912).

The joint traditions begun with Locke and Descartes first influenced the natural sciences, but eventually became the way that inquirers in the human sciences also looked at research. This mindset, that is, the positivist mindset came to dominate research and evaluation within the human sciences and education.

The naturalist (phenomenological/hermeneutic) challenges

Another view, shaped by the philosophical writings of Dilthey (1988 [1923]), Heidegger (1962 [1923]), Merleau-Ponty (1962), Winch (1990 [1958]) Gadamer (1975) and articulated for researchers by the likes of Lincoln and Guba (1981), Harré (1986, 1989), Westerman (2004) and Yanchar (2006) among others, presents an understanding of humans as actors who within limits are imitators of projects and responders to the world in ways that are not always expected or controlled. Thus philosophers and researchers provide the perspective for the interpretative stance regarding inquiry.

Although Wilhelm Wundt's work in social psychology (see Rieber and Robinson (2001) for an overview) included studies using Dilthey's anthropological/ phenomenological approach, psychological and much of educational research remained in the shadow of the positivist and quantitative framework. George Herbert Mead (1903, 1913) and the Chicago School began to break the dominance of the positivist research paradigm in the human sciences (see Joas (1997) for a comprehensive examination of Mead's contribution).

The two paradigms as model for research

In Table 2.3 the two-paradigm arguments are presented side-by-side. As can be seen, these two paradigms have different positions on each of the philosophical questions: ontology, epistemology, logic, teleology, and ethics, with related implications for scholarly inquiry. These paradigms are indications of the way we see the world in general and therefore also the way we engage in research. If our views remain unarticulated, the effects of the worldview are not lessened by not knowing, but we will be less able to anticipate research problems or to solve those that they come across.

Reflecting on any of these questions will help us to see how a worldview influences research. As stated above, we all have implicit or unarticulated worldviews. Our contention is that it is helpful for us as scholarly inquirers to make at least some of our worldview explicit in an effort at better understanding our own views of how the world works and how we understand the world and ourselves as participants in it. Self-awareness, we argue, is a helpful tool for everyone involved in research and evaluation. The more we know about our own perspective the more thoughtfully we can engage in scholarly inquiry.

Table 2.3 Comparing the two paradigms.

Naturalist paradigm	Positivist paradigm
Within limits, humans construct reality by interpreting it	Reality is independent of the human observer.
Admissible evidence is generated from both our tacit understanding and tangible accounts of experience	Admissible evidence is observable and tangible.
There is a mutual influence between the inquirer and the subject of the inquiry. The interactivity makes pure objectivity impossible.	An inquiry can be conducted with minimal influence on the subject of the investigation. Pure objectivity can be approached.
Claims of consistent lawful, cause-and -effect relationships in human relational world must be tentative.	Carefully designed projects can lead to lawful and predictable relationships in the human and natural world.

What your answers to these questions are can be said to constitute your worldview. Keeping in mind this background and your own answers from Research Exercise 1.1, we are now ready to begin a discussion of some of the issues that have been contested regarding two different orientations to research, often called paradigms. Take a minute and work through the first of many research exercises.

Research exercise 2.2: Understanding the importance of worldviews to research

On a sheet of paper, write down your initial answer to the ontology question, that is, what is the nature of reality. Don't worry about being philosophical as you write – just write your thoughts more or less off the top of your head. Now, pick a partner from the class. Share your answers to the ontology questions.

How similar and different where your answers?

What elements of your answers were the same or very similar?

Now, working alone for a moment, place yourself a little ahead of time in the class as you start to formulate a research question. Here are two questions a research project might address: These questions, I would argue, come from two different worldviews. What was the learning outcome from this class? How can I better understand what students are learning in the class? Which question do you think fits into which of worldview? Use Table 2.2 to help you in making your choice.

Now talk with your partner about how you might go about answering both questions. The point here is to use what you already know to help you better understand some of the issues to be raised in this and later chapters, not to have a definitive or even a solid answer to the question.

Naturalist paradigm versus the positivist paradigm

In this section, I challenge the coupling of naturalistic and qualitative as well as the coupling of quantitative and positivist. I begin by presenting some of the questions that are in contention, that is, questions that are a part of the ongoing debate about how or even if, research methods may be combined. Many of the questions are philosophical in nature, that is, they are questions about epistemology.

In addressing the philosophical issues regarding research, we have divided the presentation into two distinct areas: First, the debate about qualitative and quantitative inquiry within the context of the naturalist and positivist paradigms and second, a definitional and philosophical construction of the nature of interpretative inquiry. These two areas are addressed separately as it is difficult to understand the nature of interpretative inquiry if the discussion is not situated within the larger two paradigms debate.

I begin with a definition of research paradigms. There are two widely used definitions of paradigm. In one definition a paradigm is an example or pattern of something, that is, a model. In the second definition, a paradigm is also a worldview underlying the theories and methodology of a particular scientific subject. Both definitions are sometimes used in discussions of research (see for example, Siegel 2009); however, when researchers write about the paradigm wars, they are most often using the second definition. I will use the second definition (paradigm as worldview) exclusively. A worldview, that is, how one sees and understands the world, is likely to have an important, perhaps profound, influence on how research is conducted. To take one example, if a person understands reality as a mirror reflecting what is in the world, that person will have a different perspective on research than if she believes that the world is, at least in part, influenced by personal experiences and knowledge, i.e. reality is constructed. Let's look at how these worldviews might express themselves in an actual research project. With a view of the world that allows one to directly translate what one sees as what is, in other words, what I see is the essence of what exists in the world, then I can take a phenomenon, say a classroom, and break it down into discrete elements, some of which are held constant and others of which are manipulated. I can measure each of the elements and provide a picture of what a classroom is like that presents it as it is. If on the other hand, I see the classroom as constructed by its individual members, I would be more interested in how individual students and the teacher understand the classroom from their perspective, that is, how they construct a meaning for the classroom as a lived experience. Issues such as the nature of reality as well as others will be presented in some detail shortly; our point here is merely to show how a paradigm, a worldview, might influence research.

It will be necessary to sort through some (but not all) of the paradigm issues or questions. Like the reader, I have struggled with understanding and addressing the issues raised by these philosophical questions. That struggle informs this book so allow me to provide a little personal perspective on the two paradigms approach. My struggle is both philosophical and practical. The philosophical question comes first. Lincoln and Guba (1985) made a case for the two-paradigm model. It was a compelling argument, if one accepted the premises, and I took that stand in *Beginning Qualitative Research* (Maykut and Morehouse 1994). The two paradigms are incompatible. One cannot use research methods, or even make a case that researchers working in the different paradigms can communicate with each other; the two paradigms are that different. However, I now think that this perspective is wrongheaded, in that the most natural and human scientists and researchers are on the naturalist side of the equation. Perhaps it was even an unintentional misrepresentation for political or pedagogical reasons (more on that later).

Let us now briefly examine the philosophical underpinnings of the two-paradigm approach. It can correctly be argued that there is a stark difference between the position of the logical positivists and the naturalists. Our adoption of Lincoln and Guba's orientation on the paradigm illustrates the differences and implicitly points to why research done in the two different paradigms does not and cannot fit together.

Shortly after *Beginning Qualitative Research* (1994) was published I was presenting several workshops on qualitative research at the University of Melbourne. A major focus of the presentation was on orienting the audience regarding the importance of understanding the philosophical underpinnings of qualitative research. A major part of my approach was to explore the two paradigms and their relationship to conducting research. In a question and answer session at the end of the presentation, an audience member said, "I like your efforts to examine the philosophic background for qualitative research, but isn't there some way that the two paradigms can come together, or some way to allow qualitative and quantitative research to inform each other?" My response was "Yes, but I don't know how to do it." I have been struggling to answer that question ever since. I now realize that I focused almost exclusivelyon the first part of the question, that is, blending the two paradigms or making complementary the positivist and naturalist paradigms. I now think that I should have devoted my thinking to the second part of the question, i.e. how to connect quantitative and qualitative research projects. The two questions are related, but how they were related was my dilemma.

It was helpful for me as a qualitative researcher to sort out the issues relating to these research paradigms. Without an awareness of the two paradigms and their affect of scholarly inquiry, I would not have been able to rethink and eventually respond to the question asked many years ago in Melbourne. As stated above, I now realize that the two paradigms were not the problem as I had originally thought. I now think the two paradigms were straw-persons. In practice most researchers are oriented toward a naturalist position. So the issue now becomes how can inquirers blend quantitative and qualitative data in a single study? This new issue is more amenable to a solution.

A little explanation is required to understand how quantitative, experimental research fits on the naturalistic side of the paradigm equation. Michael Westerman (2006) provides a partial answer. He argues that mainstream quantitative researchers are in error when they claim to follow the principles of positivism.

> Notwithstanding nearly ubiquitous references to "operationalizing" variables and hypotheses about relations between variable, quantitative research procedures as they are actually employed do not objectively translate theoretical ideas about constructs and processes into meaning-free language about procedures. Instead, interpretation plays a crucial role.
>
> (Westerman 2006: 191)

Jürgen Habermas provided a philosophical perspective on combining qualitative and quantitative inquiry. Following Dilthey, he argued that understanding, as opposed to explication, begins with the fusion of the experiential and the theoretical. In *Understanding the Human Sciences*

> [w]hat we have first is experienced unity. Distinguishing its individual factors comes afterwards. This brings about a very great difference between the methods through which we study psychic life, history, and society, and those through which the knowledge of nature is achieved
>
> (Dilthey cited in Habermas 1971: 45)

Qualitative and quantitative methods may be combined with this sense of unity of experience leading to understanding. By beginning with the unity of experience the inquirer provides a basis for both context and interpretation.

Westerman (2005), in the spirit of Dilthey and Habermas, argues that most quantitative researchers focus on the meaning of psychological and educational phenomena. He sees this orientation of most quantitative researchers as consistent with what philosophers of sciences have been saying for some time. Along with philosophers like Peter Winch (1990 [1958]), who argues for a non-positivist outlook for the human or social sciences, Westerman argues that this non-positivist perspective is even true of hard sciences such as physics. He goes on to state "Unfortunately, when psychologists subscribe to the official picture of quantitative research, they are adopting a misunderstanding of themselves as investigators on the basis of an outmoded philosophical viewpoint" (2005: 191). Measurement is one of the areas of psychology that is rife with meaning parading as objectivity. He cites Likert-scales and Q-sorts as technical machinery that masks meaning. Self-reports and "operationally-defined" behavior codes also make his list of meaning-oriented measures. Westerman also makes the point that the use of statistics does not make something consistent with the positivist perspective, if our "examination of the phenomena is *not* mathematical in nature" (emphasis in original, 2006: 194).

Stephen Yanchar (2006: 212) continues the argument of Westerman (2006) in the same issue of *New Ideas in Psychology* stating

> some quantitative strategies when carefully interpreted and employed, can make integral contributions of the meaningful study of human action in context and provide potentially useful resources for the development of novel questions, theories, arguments and problem solution within a contextual framework.

Qualitative and quantitative research working together

Both Westerman (2005, 2006) and Yanchar (2006) make a case for scholarly inquiry in the social sciences in particular, being contextual and interpretative. Following our framing of the research paradigms as being positivist or naturalist, they are both on the naturalist side of the equation. If one is on the naturalist side of the equation, than the only part of my problem to be solved is how can we get quantitative and qualitative data working together on the same study? The answer to this question falls into two parts: (1) general concerns regarding compatibility, and (2) an orientation that does justice to humans as agents and meaning-makers.

Compatibility

Compatibility is being able to coexist without conflict. Applied to scholarly inquiry this means that the data as gathered and as analyzed must support an answer to the research question that shares a common thread. This thread should be coherent and have philosophical integrity.

Some researchers such as Michael Q. Patton and others (Patton 1990; Firestone 1990) have argued that the primary, perhaps the only thing that a scholarly inquirer needs to pay attention to is the research questions; however, that is not our stance. The task of the scholarly inquirer, according to these authors, is to find out if the question will be well answered by qualitative and quantitative data. That position is unsatisfying on two levels. First it is not very helpful to the researcher struggling to find a way to mix data collection and analysis, as it provides no help in answering the question as to which projects lend themselves to using mixed data to address an important research or evaluation question. Second, it is unsatisfying on the level of philosophy, that is, it fails to address what we see as challenging questions as to how different methods can fit together into a coherent whole.

The way we address the first question of how does one investigate a problem using mixed methods of data collection and analysis is to look to an anti-Cartesian worldview, specifically as a phenomenological worldview. A look back at Chart 2.2 will provide some beginning direction. The project must be open to interpretation. What does it mean to interpret? To interpret something is to understand an action, mood, or way of behaving; it is to give a particular meaning or significance to that action, mood, or behavior.

If we are on the naturalist side of the paradigm divide, we see a connection between ourselves as observers and what we are observing. Gergen and Gergen (2000: 1026) state:

> there is no means of privileging any particular account on the grounds of its unique match to the world. The intelligibility of our accounts of the world are derived not from the world itself, but from our immersion within a tradition of cultural practices we inherit from previous generations.

We are a part of the world we are observing; we can't stand above it with a "God's eye view." If there are no privileged views of the world, this complicates the question about interpretation. One thing is clear; one is likely to investigate a problem using different methods of data collection and analysis from those one would if the world could be seen in an objective manner. However, not all mixing of data are appropriate. One element that we hold to be essential in interpretative scholarly inquiry is a focus on practice, particularly practice in progress, that is, *in medias res*.

Stephen Yanchar and David Williams (2006) argue that methods are based on common assumptions about "the phenomena to be investigated" (p. 4).

> If the theoretical nature of one method precludes that of another, then no mixing can take place that does not either collapse into incoherence or involves a framework of assumptions that integrates the methods and renders their combined data coherent and interpretable.

> (ibid.)

They argue that methods cannot be separated from theoretical concerns, or that we have been referring to philosophical issues. Within that context, they propose five guidelines for mixing qualitative and quantitative studies:

1   contextual sensitivity,
2   creativity,
3   conceptual awareness,
4   coherence, and
5   critical reflection.

Let us look briefly at each of these proposals.

Contextual sensitivity is perhaps the most accessible idea. Simply stated it asks researchers and evaluators to be aware that their projects are shaped by theoretical assumptions so it is paramount to examine closely how methods of data collection and analysis fit together. Creativity asks investigators to use whatever tools might help to fruitfully and thoroughly interrogate a given subject matter including combinations of quantitative and qualitative data, action research, developmental studies, historical studies, and theoretical and philosophical studies (Yanchar and Williams 2006: 9). Coherence to a scholarly inquirer means to "work in a reasonably coherent manner so that theories, questions, methods, data analyses, and criteria for success form meaningful and interpretable accounts" (ibid.). Critical reflection asks researchers and evaluators to look at whether their assumptions about research are fallible, alterable, and in need of critical examination. These ideas will be further developed in Chapter 3, "The interpretative stance."

Humans as agents and meaning-makers

We humans are agents and meaning-makers both in our daily lives and as scholarly inquirers. That means that if we are a part of a group that is being studied we have to be considered as actors or agents and not as subjects to be manipulated, and as persons who give meaning to our actions. This also holds true if we are the observers, if we are the researchers.

A project on the naturalistic side of the equation must also look to people's words and actions. Whether the words and actions are preserved in a story, a narrative, or aggregated using a mathematical or statistical procedure, the focus remains on the meaning of these words and actions – especially meaning as understood by the persons involved in the study. Peter Winch (1990 [1958]) offers a perspective on what it means to focus on words and actions that are open to interpretation. Central to our understanding of how to conduct scholarly inquiry in an interpretative mode is the idea of voluntary action.

> Voluntary behaviour is behaviour to which there is an alternative. Since understanding something involves understanding its contradictory, someone who, with understanding, performs X must be capable of envisaging the possibility of doing not-X. This is not an empirical statement but a remark about what is involved in the concept of doing something with understanding. Consider now as observer, O, of N's behaviour. If O wants to predict how N is going to act he must familiarize himself with the concepts in terms of which N is viewing the situation; having done this he may, from his knowledge of N's character, be able to predict with great confidence what decision N is going to take. But the notions which O uses to make his prediction are nonetheless compatible with N's taking a different decision from that predicted by him.
>
> (Winch 1990 [1958]: 91)

This quote from Winch also relates to interactivity of the observed and the observer. This interaction plays itself out on two levels. First, as we know from physics (the Heisenberg principle in particular), to observe something is to change it. This is even more germane in the human sciences (Winch 1990 [1958]; Smith 2009). Additionally, there is the issue of prediction. As Winch writes, predictions are, from an interpretative stance, dependent on understanding the perspective of the observed person and not exclusively on the data being observed.

> If this happens it does not necessarily follow that O has made a mistake in his calculations; for the whole point about a decision is that a given set of "calculations" may lead to any one of a set of different outcomes. This is quite different from predictions in the natural sciences, where a falsified prediction always implies some sort of mistake on the part of the predictor; false or inadequate data, faulty calculation, or defective theory
>
> (Winch 1990 [1958]: 90)

Smith (2009) in like manner sees rules for action central to understanding human actions; however, he also acts as deontic, i.e. based on obligation-permission-proscription. He states, "the deontic obligation to do X can validly coexist with the non-performance of X" (p. 240). Winch and Smith are in agreement that predictions based exclusively on past observations do not necessarily hold regardless of how careful and accurate the observations are.

Svend Brinkmann (2009) argues that social life and mental life are dependent on normative rule following, and that facts and values are interwoven in rich ethical descriptions. He write that values, that is, "What am I to do" in MacIntyre's words, are embedded in stories and storied communities.

> Actions are not only situated in the context of practice, but also in the context of human life, i.e. actions are at once constitutive of, and constituted by, narrative lived by the person within some community of story-telling: the key for men is not about their authorship; I can only answer the question "What am I to do?" if I can answer the prior question "of what story or stories do I find myself a part? (MacIntyre 1985: 216)."
>
> (Brinkmann 2009: 11)

Understanding the world of human interaction is the study of complex interacting and multidirectional influences between and among human beings, who are themselves situated in social, economic, and political contexts, which preclude linear cause-effect relationships. Even an area that many psychologist have seen as most personal and private, that is, thinking or cognition, is now seen by many psychologists as shared. Thinking is seen by many psychologist as distributed cognition, co-constructed knowledge, situated cognition and extended minds (Bruner 1990; Perkins 1995: Susswein and Racine 2009). Westerman (2005) and Bickhard (2009) among others argue that the way of understanding human interaction is from an interactionist perspective.

Values play a part in all research

Values are embedded in all scholarly inquiry. Two definitions of value are relevant here. First, a value is something that is important or precious to a person or group of people.

Second, a value is a set of principles or standards that a person holds. It seems obvious that we only research or evaluate topics that are of value to us. As research and evaluation are rigorous and time consuming, we choose our topic with great care. Interpretative inquirers "wear their values on their sleeve" so to speak, that is, they are open about the influences of their values in the selection of topics for research, in their choice of methods for data collection and analysis, and in their methods of presenting the results to a larger audience.

This public recognition of the role of values follows through to the adoption and application of principles and standards for research. While principles and standards are upheld as a part of any research project, interpretative researchers are perhaps more conscious, more public, about the role of values. The obvious principles include the general guidelines for research included in discipline-based ethical standards. Additionally, qualitative research places the person at the center of the study; it places them as participants and contributors to the study and not as subjects to be manipulated.

Defining interpretative inquiry

"Interpretative inquiry" is a term chosen to circumscribe or limit the field of scholarly inquiry to a specific type of investigation. There are many types of investigations that might include both quantitative and qualitative data. However, the research discussed here will only include those that might be called interpretative. These studies may be exclusively quantitative or qualitative or mixed method, but they share perspective on how to examine human behavior and interaction. While some of the researchers and theorists that we will include do not use the term interpretative, they all share this perspective of people and on research. Bickhard uses the term specifically and makes a case for interactionism as a way to study human phenomena. One of his articles in entitled "Interactivism: A manifesto" (2009), and in it interactivism is defined as an acceptance of the idea that reality is integrated, that is there are no isolated and independent grounds of reality, in fact, everything is process or the organization of process in Bickhard's view. Put more directly, this means that a world exists that we are born into, that we join in process. It means that we draw into the world. We are not separate Cartesian beings. Descartes saw us as disembodied minds. Both Westerman and Bickhard share an anti-Cartesian view of the world. Westerman (2005, 2006) also writes about an interpretative perspective on research. He defines interpretative behavior as referring what one person contributes to a joint activity with one or more people (2005: 22). This is a participatory model of interpersonal behavior that implies the lived experiences of agents acting within the context of meaning making.

One of Westerman's interests is articulating an understanding of the nature of interpersonal behavior (2005, 2006). In doing so, he looks to the phenomenological and pragmatic (that is, Deweyan) critique of Descartes and a functional perspective that looks to how a person's actions contribute to doing something with other people (2005). "Instead of taking as its basic view the Cartesian framework of subjects separate from the world, this perspective takes as its starting point the person involved in practical activities in the world" (Westerman 2005: 20). In colorful language Westerman helps us understand the move away from the Cartesian perspective by writing that humans are understood not as contemplating the apple but, using Merleau-Ponty's term, *involved subjects*, that is, we begin our understanding of people as looking at them "eating the apple, selling it, and using it for the moment as a paperweight to keep papers from blowing away" (ibid.). This colorful example helps the reader turn around a way we think about the study of psychology, that is, it moves us away from thinking about entities and toward thinking about human interaction. Westerman argues meaningful, organized activities become the lens through which we understand feelings, cognitions, and behaviors. Some recent critiques of psychology (Brinkmann 2009; Bickhard 2009; Susswein and Racine 2009; Bruner 1990, 1996; Cole *et al.* 1997; Ragoff 2003; Harré and van Langenhove 1999) have focused on looking at the person as a part of the social world rather than from a subject-object split. As psychologists and educators, we need to understand the actions of persons within the context of an interaction with another person. Specifically "We cannot start with individual behaviours and build up an account of what goes on between people, because these behaviors must be viewed as contributions to the larger activity" (Westerman 2005: 22).

Pulling all this discussion of interpretative inquiry together, I define interpretative inquiry as quantitative, qualitative, and mixed method research that sees humans as agents who act with others in a social and cultural context. Within this perspective, our understanding of humans cannot be separated from their social and cultural world that is always in process. My perspective begins with an understanding of how we study human beings. As stated in the introduction, Bruner writes that the proper study of humans focuses an action, meaning-making, and agency. Stated somewhat differently, interpretative research seeks to understand human interaction by exploring these three orientations (action, meaning, and agency) and using hermeneutic methods as the framework for research in education and psychology. Bruner sees psychology as organized around meaning-making and meaning-using processes that connect man to culture. "By virtue of participation in culture, meaning is rendered *public* and *shared*" (Bruner 1990: 12–13). Interpretative inquiry seeks to understand shared meaning and shared concepts that are created within discourse and activities that allow us to negotiate differences in meaning and interpretation.

Making a case for interpretative inquiry

In some ways the definition of interpretative inquiry begins to make the case for conducting research from that perspective. If we are to focus on agency, action, and meaning-making and look to practice *in medias res*, this eliminates many potential studies and forces us to rethink others. Put another way, the reason that interpretative inquiry ought to be done is that questions of interaction between and among people who are engaged in joint practice are important to education and psychology. To take just two examples, one each from psychology and education, I argue that it is more valuable to teachers and educators to understand how a particular practice works in a classroom than it is to find out if "x" curriculum yields a higher score in the aggregate than "y" curriculum. While both research projects are of value, gaining a detailed picture of the curriculum, the teacher, and the students as they engage with the material is more informative to present and future classroom teachers than the latter. To take an example from psychology, a study of an interpersonal relationship between therapist and patient will be more helpful to the therapist than some general commentary comparing this orientation to that orientation.

Summary

Interpretative inquiry is an approach to research and evaluation that emphasizes a phenomenological perspective that sees humans as born into history. Persons are embodied and embedded in a complex world. Further, knowledge cannot be reduced to a single privileged perspective nor be easily reducible to cause and effect. As such, we are required to understand the world as being in process, rather than as a complete entity that can be broken into small pieces to be manipulated and "objectified." We are agents who act on the world as we seek meaning. This holds for scholarly inquirers as well as ordinary persons in the day-to-day of living. It holds for the observed as well as the observer. The interpretative approach to research can be placed on the naturalistic side of the two-paradigm perspective on the worldview of researchers. Table 2.4 summarizes this stance.

Table 2.4 Interpretative research stance.

Philosophical question	Interpretative research stance
What do we believe about the nature of reality?	Human beings construct reality by interpreting their perspectives on it. Thus, it is likely that for any given instance, more than more reality – truth – exists. The world is best understood as an entity I am born into and can only be given meaning as an ongoing process from which I cannot separate myself.
What are the ways of finding out knowledge?	In constructing our realities, what counts as "admissible knowledge" is generated from our tacit understanding and tangible accounts of experience. What people see, hear, feel, think, say, and do matters as we inquire into any human phenomenon. As a part of my lived-experiences as a human being, I am invited to participate, to understand, to figure things out in the middle of things.
What is the relationship between the inquirer and that which is being inquired into?	The inquirer and what is to be inquired into interact to influence the outcome of the inquiry. The interactivity makes pure objectivity possible. As an inquirer I am a part of what I am looking into. While I can't separate myself from the world, I can nonetheless work toward a fair but always tentative understanding of the phenomena under investigation.
What roles do values play in understanding the world?	Values influence how we go about understanding and inquiring about the world and the conclusions we accept as knowledge. Values are an inherent quality of human inquiry. I am a valuing person. My values are a part of my investigation, but by articulating them and making them public I can engage in careful investigations.
Are causal linkages possible?	We are highly suspect of claims of consistent, lawful, cause-and-effect relationships in the human relational world. We assume that there is a complex interacting and multidirectional influence between and among human beings, who are themselves situated in social, economic, and political contexts, which preclude linear cause-effect relationship. Multidirectionality can be understood if examined as fluid.
What can one learn from inquiries in the social sciences?	Meaningful and in-depth understanding is the aim of social science. After an in-depth understanding of a phenomenon is provided, transferability is up to the reader. Relational connections are always in progress but scholarly inquiry can provide insight into the workings of individual relational practices and thus provide a partial and tentative, but nonetheless helpful picture of important interactions.

The next chapter will provide an understanding of the way interpretative inquirers go about their work as they engage in research and evaluation projects. "The interpretative stance" provides more details of the interpretative inquirer in action. It will provide the potential interpretative inquirer with a final set of moorings before we begin the hands-on chapters that will take the beginning interpretative inquiry from initial thoughts about a project to preparing a completed project for publication.

Chapter 3

The interpretative stance

Inquiry *in medias res*

This chapter explores the implications of agency, action, and meaning within the context of the researcher and the focus of inquiry being "in the middle of things." As I have argued in the previous chapter, education and psychology are not well served by the methods of the natural sciences, as these laws are deterministic. Human acts cause and are caused by events outside themselves; however, thought, desire, and voluntary action cannot be brought under deterministic laws, as physical phenomena can. Interpretative inquirers study human action. To understand human action means to examine the influences of outside events (causes) and individuals who in the process of making choices change us and are changed by us. This is what I am calling the interpretative stance.

A stance is the attitude of a person or organization toward something – a standpoint. This stance focuses on consequences in action and interaction. "This does not mean any events that are undetermined or unpredictable; it is only events as described in the vocabulary of thought and action that resist incorporation into a closed deterministic system" (Davidson 1994: 80). People and human relationships cannot be studied using the same methods as physical objects. "When we attribute a desire, a belief, a goal, an intention, or meaning to an agent, we necessarily operate within a system of concepts in part determined by the structure of beliefs and desires of the agent himself" (ibid.).

What I will establish in this chapter is the position or stance of interpretative inquiry in the social or human sciences. More metaphorically, I will provide a patch of firm ground for the interpretative researcher and evaluator to stand on, that is, an orientation for the interpretative inquirer.

Why is it important to establish a stance for the interpretative inquirer? I argue that there is a phenomenon that I call the "agentic paradox." The agentic paradox can be stated as follows. Most of us, either consciously and unconsciously, see ourselves as agents, but when we conduct research we strip those we wish to study of the very properties that we see as most essential to our persona as researchers, namely intentionality, forethought, self-reactiveness, and self-reflection, that is to say, agency.

The concern is that as researchers and evaluators our tendency is to see the persons we are trying to find out more about as objects to be studied, rather than as persons who are agents like us. The cultural framework of researchers is that of a laboratory. The lab is the default model of a scientist. It continues to play a role in how we see ourselves as inquirers. We want to be good researchers and the model of a good researcher is that scientist in the lab. While we know, on one level, that people and human relationships are not the same as molecular relationships, we nonetheless value the "objectivity" of the chemist or the biologist in the lab.

Most of us have little experience with interpretative inquiry, with seeing our research participants as agents, so concerns and problems are likely to be seen through the lens of our previous work or the work that we have read and reviewed as consumers of research and evaluation. Faced with questions about how to solve a problem in our research or evaluation project, we are likely to turn to what we know, or think we know, about research as previously conducted. In some cases, this would mean falling back on a positivist perspective, rather than asking how this question can be addressed to focus on action, agency, and meaning within a relational context regardless of the data collection and data analysis methods we use.

Now that we know the problem, what is the solution? I argue that the solution is to establish a firm grounding in interpretative inquiry. Here are some of the key elements of interpretative inquiry that inquirers ought to pay close attention to. An interpretative inquirer looks to the following: Understanding action in context, understanding relationships among and between actors, and understanding how agents engage with each other and with the world. I will elaborate on each one during the rest of this chapter.

In order to gain a better perspective on the interpretative stance, a couple of additional conceptual issues still need to be resolved. The first issue is regarding the larger context of inquiry. John Dewey makes a case for a larger rethinking of how we conceptualize research. He argues that inquirers need to address three issues: the Plotinian temptation, the Galilean purification, and the asomatic attitude (Boisvert 1998: 5). The Plotinian temptation is the idea that all is one, in other words, inquiry should lead to unity. The temptation stems from our understanding of the natural sciences, that is, we understand the entire physical world to be one. While this may be true at the atomic level, it is also reasonable to see the physical world at the molecular level. Dewey favors the study of humans on the molecular level where harmony within diversity is the preferred viewpoint. From this perspective unity is not an achievable outcome nor does it have explanatory value. Dewey's anti-Plotinian position is consistent with the idea of multiple realities and divergent perspectives discussed by Lincoln and Guba (1985) and Denzin and Lincoln (2000) among others (Skate 2006, 2010; Taylor 1995). The way to deal with these multiple realities and divergent perspectives is to find the harmony between them, not to distill them into a single reality. The Galilean purification is the tendency among inquirers to remove oneself from the topic of study. Dewey advocated for an approach to inquiry based on ordinary lived experience. As inquirer and participants, we cannot be seen as entirely separate, there is a commonality between an inquirer and the object of the inquiry. We are a part of what we study. My point about the agentic paradox is similar to Dewey's Galilean purification. Third, Dewey saw inquiry as embodied rather than as an asomatic experience. The embodied experience places the individual within an historic and physical world. While no one claims to be a disembodied mind, philosophers and non-philosophers alike sometimes talk as though this were possible. Dewey's plea for an embodied orientation to inquiry challenges that unspoken assumption. In many ways, this is an extension of our everyday lived experience; it places emphasis on an embodied intelligence that does not cut the head off from the body. Understanding ourselves, and those we are engaging as participants in our studies, are essential criteria for interpretative inquiry; it is an additional way in which inquirers orientate themselves to the world. To summarize, Dewey sees inquirers as agents who are embodied, seek harmony from divergent perspectives, and are grounded in lived experiences.

What Dewey's writings add to the discussion of agency is the idea that agents should not be seen as independent, unconnected Cartesian entities, but rather as agents-in-the-world. This point is also consistent with Michael Westerman's perspective on interpersonal behavior (2005). Westerman, like Dewey, takes an anti-Cartesian stand on understanding the world, especially the interpersonal world, though he draws on the works of Merleau-Ponty, Wittgenstein, and Heidegger for his support. In his essay on defining interpersonal behavior (Westerman 2005) he presents a participatory model for interpersonal behavior. "According to this model, *interpersonal behavior refers to a person's contribution to doing something with other people*" (p. 22, emphasis in the original). Following Merleau-Ponty, he looks to involved subjectivity, that is, our understanding of a behavior begins with the person doing the behavior (p. 20). "Dovetailing" is one of the ways to capture the ideas of feeling, cognitions, and behaviors in the lived world of meaningful, organized activities. Westerman argues for a perspective of involved subjectivity that is characterized by the "psychological phenomena *embedded* in the *social* world" (p. 21). This stance directs the inquirer's "attention to the *context of exchange* within which the behavior occurs" (p. 22, emphasis in the original).

Stephen Yanchar extends the idea of inquiry as a non-Cartesian enterprise when he explores the idea of contextual-quantitative inquiry.

> [S]ome quantitative strategies, when carefully interpreted and employed, can make integral contributions to the meaningful study of human actions in context and provide a potentially useful resource for the development of novel questions, theories, arguments, and problem solutions within a contextual framework.
>
> (Yanchar 2006: 212)

Key features of agency as it applies to inquiry

Agency, as discussed earlier, is one of the key elements of interpretative inquiry as both inquirers and those who are the subject of inquiry are agents. This relationship is the core of the agentic paradox discussed above. The key features of agency (Bandura 2001) as they relate to inquiry, fall into four categories: (1) intentionality, (2) forethought, (3) self-reactiveness, and (4) self-reflectiveness.

A brief look at each of these categories of agency is in order. The idea of intentionality goes at least back to Franz Brentano (cf. Flanagan 1984). A simple understanding of intentionality is that it is the relationship between mental acts and the external world; intentionality is a mental phenomenon that is "about" something (Brentano 1995). Bandura's use of intentionality is consistent with Brentano's definition. "An intention is a representation of a future course of action to be performed. It is not simply an expectation or prediction of future action but a proactive commitment to bringing them about" (Bandura 2001: 6). The point here is that a part of being an agent is to have intentions, mental representations of desires, hopes, fears, and beliefs.

In Dewey's writing on agency what is of particular importance is his thinking on forethought. Forethought is a learned behavior as "[t]he natural tendency of man is to do something at once" (Dewey 1988: 178). This tendency is checked by thought. "Thinking," Dewey writes, "has well been called deferred action" (ibid.). Dewey argues that thinking is a stopping of action in that one can think something through without an action occurring. Our thoughts, therefore, are revocable in that we can replay a mental act, but not a physical act. He goes on to write that "deferred action is present exploratory action" (ibid.). Bandura examines the same idea that he calls forethought, writing, "Through the exercise of forethought, people motivate themselves and guide their actions in anticipation of future events" (2001: 7). A part of the agentic stance is to have a reflective temperament. Thus deferred action, whether by inquirers or participants in an inquiry, is a form of forethought.

Agency not only involves planning and forethought, but also motivation and self-regulation as well. An agent is involved in deliberation and decision-making but must also shape an appropriate course of action. The agent motivates and regulates the execution of their choices and action plans (Bandura 2001: 8).

Each of these features is internal to inquirers and participants in the study and therefore essential in understanding an interpretative project. Understanding both sides of agency in an inquiry is an important framework as we begin planning and eventually implementing a project. One of those internal elements is reflectiveness.

Agency, as a part of what it means to be a person, is also a social process. Joas credits George Herbert Mead with the idea that what we are as individual human beings attached to and rooted in the social structure (Joas 1997: 57). Mead argues that one's personhood is, in fact, a social construction. Autonomy, according to Mead, requires for its emergence a reshaping of social life, which must be so organized that free self-determination of all is both possible and necessary (Joas 1997: 35). This socially creative but individual agent is at the core of our understanding of the interpretative inquirer.

Interpretative theory informs research with its focus on a shared world in which both the inquirer and the participants in the study live. Both the inquirer and the participants are trying to understand the same phenomena.

Table 3.1 Core features of agency for the inquirer and participant.

Core features of agency	Inquirer	Participant
Intentionality: a representation of a future course of action to be performed (Bandura 2001: 6; Dewey 1926)	Inquirers create a mental picture, a plan for the research or evaluation in which they will engage	Participants learn about the nature of the project and anticipate ways they will be involved in the study
Forethought: the way one motivates oneself and guides their actions in anticipation of future events (Bandura 2001: 7; Dewey 1926)	Inquirers anticipate what they will gain from and what they will contribute to the research or evaluation activities	Participants anticipate what they will gain from and what they will contribute to the research or evaluation activities
Self-reactiveness: performance comparison with personal goals and standards that direct action (Bandura 2001: 8)	As the project proceeds, the inquirers compare the progress of the inquiry to their understanding of the standards of the research community and their own stated goals	As the project proceeds the participants compare what they anticipated as their involvement to their actual involvement in the project.
Self-reflectiveness: the capacity to reflect upon oneself and the adequacy of one's thoughts and actions (Bandura 2001: 10).	The inquirers ask themselves: Are we up to the task as we conceived?	The participants ask themselves: Are we contributing in the ways that we anticipated?

Research exercise 3.1: Core features of agency

Intentionality

Before we begin an inquiry we imagine ourselves engaged in the task. Take a few minutes and think about a project that you would like to investigate. What does the setting look like? Who is present? How are you feeling? What are your thoughts about starting the project? These are your intentions, the contents of your thought about research. Intentionality means that you cannot think about research in the abstract – it will always be about something.

Forethought

An extension of intentionality is forethought. How will the project unfold? What problems might emerge? What might the result of the project be? How it will be received? It is also important to be aware that the participants are asking themselves about how things will unfold, and what the reaction of others (namely the inquirer) will be to them.

Self-reactiveness

How does this project compare to other projects that you have read about or perhaps even conducted? Looking to the other side of the divide, so to speak, how do the participants see themselves performing in this inquiry?

Self-reflectiveness

Are you up to the task? This is a self-reflective question. While it may seem self-evident in this exercise that one engages in self-reflection as a part of an inquiry project, this process is not often a conscious part of the inquiry process. Perhaps even more importantly, we do not generally give the participants in the inquiry the same self-reflective perspective.

Bandura (2001) also writes about modes of agency. He argues that many things people seek to understand about the world are not achievable by individual effort but are achievable with socially interdependent effort. If we work with others, we can understand what we cannot understand on our own. Bandura defines collective agency as people's shared beliefs in their collective power to produce results based on their shared intentions, knowledge, and skills (p. 14). Of particular interest to interpretative inquirers is the collective mode. The collective mode "is people acting conjointly on a shared belief, not a disembodied group mind that is doing the cognizing, aspiring, motivating, and regulating" (ibid.). If people see themselves as conjointly solving a problem, they might be considered to be a collective research team. "Thinking has well been called deferred action ... deferred action is present exploratory action" (Dewey 1926: 178).

Key features of activity as it applies to inquiry

Following a perspective articulated by Michael Westerman (2005) and based on what Merleau-Ponty (1962) called *involved subjectivity*, I argue that the interpretative inquirer should not see the subject of inquiry as apart from himself, but as a person with her or his own preceptions, ideas, and feelings. We begin instead with both inquirer and participant engaged in life's activities (p. 20). That is to say, the process of inquiry begins with inquirers and participants engaged in the world.

For example, human skills (perception, cognition, emotions, behavior) are incomplete. Westerman extends his argument by stating that emotions are "not isolatable ways of establishing correspondences between inner presentations and the world out there" (2005: 20), persons do not merely react to what it is the world is like. Rather, skills (perceptions, cognitions, emotions, and behaviors) are always *part* of doing things in the world. As parts of a whole, skills "dovetail" with each other and events to constitute organized activity (2005: 20–21).

John Dewey, while not often cited by research methodologists, provides many insights into the ways of interpretative inquiry. His discussion of means and ends may be particularly helpful as we explore the role of action in inquiry. Dewey sees ends as foreseen consequences that arise in the course of activities. We use ends to give added meaning to our actions and to direct actions toward a future course of action. Thus if we are to understand the action of others, we need to have some sense of their ends. "In being ends of deliberation they are redirecting pivots *in* action" (Dewey 1922: 209). Goals are means of defining and deepening the means of activity. "An end-in-view is a means in presentation; present action is not a means to a remote end" (ibid.: 210). From this perspective inquiry that is isolated, complete, or has fixed ends limits intellectual explanations (ibid.: 214).

Westerman's writes about "practical activity" in a manner that is consistent with Dewey's discussion of means and ends. Westerman sees practical activity as contextual and as incomplete.

> The notion that all human skills are incomplete helps us to see that *in order for individual behavior to contribute to creating the context of joint activity, they must dovetail with the other behaviors in the interaction in a way that creates context.*
> (Westerman 2005: 22, emphasis in the original)

For Dewey, goals and activities are intricately tied together. A goal is a way of defining and deepening the meaning of an activity. Goals or aims are not disconnected from the present. While in the present, goals or aims have a past and a future.

> Having an end or aim is thus a characteristic of *present* activity. It is the means by which the activity becomes adapted when otherwise it would be blind and disorderly, or by which it gets meaning when otherwise it would be mechanical. In a strict sense an end-in-view is a present action; present action is not a means to a remote action.
> (Dewey 1922: 209–210)

In making his point Dewey coins what to contemporary ears may seem like an unusual metaphor. He writes, "Men do not shoot because targets exist, but they set up targets in order that throwing and shooting may be more effective and significant" (1922: 210). To place this in an inquiry framework, one does not engage in a study of something because it exists, rather one creates a problem in order to better understand the world around us. He sees the enterprise of knowledge creation as related to the process of combining an occurrence with a wish to create a purpose.

The first and most important effect of this change in the understanding of action is that the dubious or unclear situation becomes *a* problem. The unknown qualities that pervade a situation are translated into objects of inquiry that locate where difficulties are and hence facilitate methods and means of dealing with them (Dewey 1922: 178).

Table 3.2 Core features of action.

Core features of action	Inquirers	Participants
Action is always interpersonal (Westerman 2005)	The inquirer and the participant engage with each other, they are not isolated actors	The participants are engaged in whatever is the topic of the inquiry as well as with the investigator
Action always takes place within a context (Westerman 2005)	Inquiry always occurs in a particular setting with particular individuals and specific times	The participants in the study are like the inquirers, involved in a particular context that contributes to their understanding as well as the inquirer's understanding of the phenomena
We are born into a world that is already in progress (Westerman 2005, 2006; Dewey 1922)	Inquiry is action in the world. It is a part of an ongoing practice of understanding. The inquirer is always already involved in meaningful practical activities (Westerman 2006)	The participants of the study, like the inquirers, are always a part of meaningful practices. (Westerman 2006)
Language is a form of action (Harré 1989; Westerman 2005)	Language as action is indispensible to the work of the inquirer. Emotions are organized action patterns	Language is one, but not the only, way we engage and understand participants

Westerman, like G. H. Mead, places action in relationship to others. Mead presents the dynamic relationship of the actor self-engaging in the complex business of understanding.

> The self acts with reference to others and is immediately conscious of the objects about it. In memory it also reintegrates the self-acting as well as the others acted upon. But besides these contents, the action with reference to the others calls out responses in the individual himself – there is then another "me" criticizing approving, and suggesting, and consciously planning, i.e. the reflective self.
>
> (Mead 1913: 3)

Our everyday activities are both interpersonal and intrapersonal as Mead states above. Research and evaluation projects are also interpersonal and intrapersonal. The following research activities provide a reminder of both of these orientations.

Research exercise 3.2: Interpersonal and intrapersonal orientations

Experiences the world as interpersonal and intrapersonal.

Think about the experiences of being a son or a daughter. Can you separate your sense of your son-ness/your daughter-ness from your understanding of and feeling about your mother or your father? While this example may seem extreme in that one cannot rhetorically or semantically separate children from parents it is equally true of any human situation that I can imagine. Can we think about Babe Ruth without thinking about baseball? Can we think about Yo-Yo Ma without thinking about music?

What does it mean to be born into a world already in progress?

Think about your experiences of seeing a newborn baby. What comes to mind? The baby's overall health and temperament – is he bright-eyed and happy? The coloring of the baby – is she pink or jaundiced? Whatever your first thoughts about the newborn are they are historical and contextual. Health and temperament are culturally defined and differently meaningful in different times and cultures. The baby's skin tone is meaningful in terms of the current state of medicine and maybe particularly related to the APGAR scale in contemporary medical settings. The point is that even these simple everyday observations can only be understood in context.

Key features of meaning-making as it applies to inquiry

What are we talking about when we talk about meaning? Things have meaning for us with relationship to a course of action. A meaningful action is a connection between a sign and an intention. John Dewey in *Human Nature and Conduct: An Introduction to Social Psychology* (1922) writes about means and ends and their relationship to meaning.

> Ends are foreseen consequences, which arise in the course of activity and are employed to give added meaning and to direct its inner course. They are in no sense ends *of* action. In being ends of *deliberation*, they are redirecting pivots *in* action.
>
> (Dewey 1922: 209)

A meaning is a relationship between two sorts of things: signs and the kinds of things they intend, express, or signify. Someone creates meaning, and understanding it requires looking at his or her action and its goal or end. We cannot understand what someone means unless we understand something of the person's history as well as the nature of their wishes. A person's actions, from this perspective, are things that happen within a context directed toward some ends. We, as humans, create meaning out of our experiences as we move toward a goal in the present moment. Thus, an inquirer trying to find out what someone means must have some picture of the experiences of the individual and know something of their goals. When we say that humans are meaning-makers, we mean that they are making sense of their experiences by placing them within a context and anticipating how present actions move them toward a set of goals. Interpretative inquirers work toward figuring out people as meaning-makers.

Table 3.3 Core features of meaning-making.

Core features of meaning-making	Inquirer	Participant
Human beings are meaning-makers and meaning-seekers	Beginning with the ideas for an inquiry to its publication, meaning-making is the leitmotif of the inquirer.	If we are to begin to understand anything about our inquiries, we must first recognize that the participants are meaning-seekers
One constructs meaning within context. This context is in past, present, and future tenses	To understand an event or a person, one must know something about their temporal world	Participant sense of time has the potential to shape the meaning of the inquiry
Aims and end construct meaning	The inquirer's aims and ends influence the nature of the inquiry	Likewise, the participant's aims and ends influence the nature of the study
Meaning occurs within the context of ongoing practice, that is, as a part of something larger than the individual act being observed or measured	From the outset, we must view stimuli, behaviors, and thoughts in terms of the role they play in meaningful practice (Westerman 2006)	The participants in the study are, like the inquirers, involved in a particular context that contributes to their understanding as well as the inquirers' understanding of the phenomena

Meaning-making occurs within the context of speech. One creates meaning as one speaks. I do not know what I mean until I say it. Merleau-Ponty states that speech does not express the thought – it completes it (Rosenthal and Bourgeois 1991). George Herbert Mead sees language as a vehicle for communicating private ideas and state of consciousness – speech is a vehicle for eliciting responses from others (ibid.). To my way of thinking this is similar to Lev Vygotsky's "assisted" learning or scaffolding. Assisted learning occurs when one person helps another person move toward completing an action or better understanding of something. Interpretative inquiry is a form of assisted learning in that the inquirer cannot find out anything without engaging the participant actively in a mutual process of probing into the phenomena under investigation.

Research exercise 3.3: Meaning-making as "assisted" learning

Interview a friend or colleague about how they recently made a decision. Conduct the interview in a casual manner – later we will work on a more professional way of conducting research interviews. As the interview unfolds, notice how the interviewee and you go back and forth clarifying, supporting, and aiding each other in understanding an answer to the question posed initially by you. This is an example of "assisted" learning and joint meaning-making.

By completing this activity, you have created a word picture of the meaning-making process as well as deepening your understanding of the relationship between meaning-making and decision-making.

Toward a reconceptualization of quantification

A well-known quote usually attributed to Einstein is "Not everything that can be counted counts, and not everything that counts can be counted" (BrainyQuote n.d.). While it may appear that what has been written so far is exclusively about qualitative inquiry, I argue that it is also true about quantitative inquiry conducted within an interpretative perspective. In order for qualitative and quantitative methods to be combined it is necessary to rethink quantitative methods in terms of an interpretative stance. What I have presented above fits fairly easily into a qualitative perspective; traditional quantitative methods do not so easily fit this stance. However, by rethinking quantitative measures as contributing to understanding agency, action, and meaning, new horizons open for the inquirer. I am going to argue here that it need not be the case that quantitative, experimental inquiry is based on a view of science that is based on reductionistic, atomistic, and determined assumptions (Yanchar 2006: 221).

As a challenge to that perspective, Stephen Yanchar presents an interpretative view of research. He argues that quantitative measures may also be seen as a part of an interpretative inquiry. This understanding of quantitative inquiry provides a foundation for my thinking on how to integrate qualitative measures with quantitative measures. Yanchar (2006) argues for a shift:

1 from self-contained variables to dynamic models,
2 from measurement to interpretation in context,
3 from internal validity to trustworthiness, and
4 from generalizability to transferability.

> Self-contained variables are for most quantitative inquirers a central tenet of research. In traditional quantitative theorizing and research, the contextual human being is involved only tangentially; the actual focus of investigation is some narrower topic of interest, typically interpreted as natural, determined process that can be decomposed into ontologically self-contained phenomena – that is, variables.
>
> (Yanchar 2006: 221)

However, humans, from the interpretative stance, are seen as agents within a specific context who have volition and create meaning. Yanchar suggests that inquirers should look to modes, actions, and experiences rather than variables or perhaps consider these concepts as variables. Variables seen this way are thus contextually related. In the same issue of *New Ideas in Psychology*, Michael Westerman (2006) points in the opposite direction arguing that many so called objective measures such as self-reports, q-sorts, and Lickert-type scales are not objective measures but are interpretative at their core. These are not cosmetic moves, but rather a deep reconceptualization of the ways one looks at quantitative methods. This, I argue, is what allows quantitative methods to be included within the interpretative stance. Seen in this light, the purpose of quantification is to clarify the parts and to organize them into themes that provide a meaningful representation of a human experience (Yanchar 2006: 221).

Yanchar's next move is to suggest that instead of looking at measurement we look at interpretation in context. Contextual quantitative research according to Yanchar is based on the "ontological assumption that human experience and action are situationally responsive and volitional" (2006: 222). From this alternative perspective, measurement can be viewed as a process whereby people are offered a language for self-interpretation and self-expression in context (ibid.). He provides an insightful example:

> Thus, scores on a test or questionnaire would be viewed as contextual self-interpretations subject to fluctuation based on the changing nature of the context and account of his or her action and experience at a given time, rather than an invariant index of a static ability.
>
> (ibid.)

Yanchar does not throw out all of the concerns of traditional quantitative researchers regarding validity. In fact he states that construct validity and test validity should be honored as long as these forms of validity are

> (a) constructed in a way that coheres with the assumptions of contextual, interpretative research; (b) that those concepts are viewed as parts of a larger argument or interpretation (based at least partly on test data) rather than transcendent properties of a test; (c) that it is understood that contextual interpretations might be unreliable according to traditional standards yet still able to communicate something meaningful about lived experience, such as when a person's action or ability fluctuates from one situation to another.
>
> (Yanchar 2006: 222)

Next, Yanchar states that interpretative inquiry should be based on a move from internal validity to trustworthiness. Internal validity is based on an atomist, linear, and objective worldview that includes a Humean sense of causation. This view is incompatible with interpretative inquiry; therefore, internal validity should be replaced with the idea of trustworthiness (p. 222). Yanchar's understanding of trustworthiness is similar to that of Lincoln and Guba who argue that if the findings are isomorphic with other views and if one is willing to act on the findings, then a finding may be considered trustworthy (1985, 2000).

Finally, Yanchar suggests that interpretative inquiry needs to move from generalizability to transferability as an alternate orientation to the positivist's perspective that a finding should be universal, that is, the finding should be applicable to the entire population. Transferability places some of the burden on the person wishing to use the research to decide if something makes sense in a new situation (Yanchar 2006). Transferability is an extension of trustworthiness.

The work of an interpretative inquirer is conducted using the following precepts:

1   interpretative stance includes the use of meaningfulness, volition, and context as tools for understanding,
2   a reading of experiences within a given context,
3   trustworthiness rather than validity as a standard for credibility, and
4   transferability as the measure of usefulness.

These principles are drawn from a hermeneutic philosophical perspective and are intended to provide a helpful viewpoint for inquirers as they engage in an interpretative study.

Summary

The interpretative stance is a conceptual framework for inquirers to have in the back of their minds as they engage in a research or evaluation project. It is intended not as a specific "how to do" set of directions (that will follow the next section, "From ideas to publication"), but rather as a tool for placing the inquirer in a frame of mind. The right frame of mind is important, as interpretative inquiry is a relatively new orientation toward research and evaluation and therefore a point of view for examining things is especially helpful. In some ways we see what we are trained to see, sometimes we only see what we are trained to see. It is my hope that by articulating the orientation of an interpretative inquirer in terms of a stance that you will be able to place yourself in a position to survey the field of inquiry with a new set of eyes; the eyes of an interpretative inquirer.

One task remains before we begin to explore the "how to," the step-by-step procedures needed to conduct an interpretative study – we need to discuss what interpretative inquiry is not. This next, short, chapter will illustrate, using some examples, the ways one can determine if something is or is not an interpretative study.

Chapter 4

A closer look at what counts as interpretative inquiry

This chapter looks at several published studies in order to provide a clearer picture for both what interpretative studies look like as well as what they do not. Why bother with an examination of interpretative versus non-interpretative inquiries? My sense is that comparing and contrasting somewhat similar things, events, or people are helpful in understanding each of those phenomena. A recent study by Holmqvist *et al.* (2007) supports my hunch. They present arguments for the importance of a theory of variation as a method of instruction. My point here is that looking at variation, in this case interpretative and non-interpretative studies, will aid in discerning interpretative studies in the future. We need to apply what we are learning here to both reading new research and evaluation projects, and to writing our own projects. A close look at variation in inquiries will aid in those efforts.

I will begin by highlighting two studies: one, an example of an interpretative qualitative study, and the other, a qualitative study that does not fit the criteria for an interpretative inquiry. Some of the writings of Kurt Fischer and Thomas Bidell (1998) along with Michael Westerman (2006) and Stephen Yanchar (2006) help provide the philosophical underpinning for the selection of these inquiries. Specifically, these studies will have a non-Cartesian orientation, focus on agency, action, and meaning-making and explore the phenomena in the middle of things.

Each study will be summarized by asking and answering the following questions: What was the purpose of the research and what were the findings? What were the data-collection methods? What were the data-analysis methods? How are the conclusions of the study presented?

Let us begin with the easiest type of article that fits the interpretative mode – a qualitative inquiry. I start here in order to set the reader off on the right footing. After you have read my summary of the article you will be invited to look at the full text of the article yourself. Below is an example of a study that falls under that interpretative rubric.

It's not always just about the grades: Exploring the achievement goal orientations of pre-med students.
(Gail Horowitz (2010) *The Journal of Experimental Education*, 78(2): 215–245.)

What is the purpose of the research and what were the findings?
Horowitz states the overall purpose of this inquiry is "to explore, delve into, and develop a better understanding of the goal orientation of a group of college level science students who were preparing for careers in medicine" (p. 218). The author

also has two more specific research questions: one relating to better understanding from a student perspective what achievement, mastery, and/or extrinsic goal orientation means, and the context in which these pre-med students adopted both mastery and extrinsic goals.

Horowitz found that there was a baseline to the perspective of the students: all students thought that grades mattered. That baseline was mediated by three different categories of goal orientation: (1) primarily mastery (I want to learn), (2) primarily extrinsic (all that really matters to me is the grade), and (3) generally extrinsic with selected mastery (I do care about grades, but …).

What were the data-collection methods?
The data was collected using a semi-structured interview schedule. The researcher interviewed each student individually. The interviews on average were ½ hour in length. She conducted all but one interview in person. Horowitz interviewed one participant by phone. The author audio-taped and transcribed all the interviews. There were 31 pre-med students in the study.

What were the data-analysis methods?
Horowitz uses data analysis methods that are especially sensitive to emerging themes. Her preliminary analysis was theoretical coding, taking handwritten notes as she played the interview tapes. These notes were placed in one of three columns: one for mastery oriented comments, one for extrinsically oriented comments and one for contradictory statements and statements fitting into both categories simultaneously. The researcher then transcribed the taped interviews. She read the transcription silently as she listened to the taped interviews. This approach allowed for an extended emersion in the data. Horowitz then looked for commonalities among students and came up with categories in which to group students.

If you wish to read another interpretative article using qualitative data collection and data analysis methods, I suggest you read "The problem-based learning process as finding and being in flow" by Terry Barrett (2010).

Research exercise 4.1: Raising questions

Examine the full text of this article to find support for, or claims that would challenge my assessment regarding the orientation of the researcher to her subjects, whether the inquiry sees pre-med students "in the middle of things" or whether the researcher sees herself in some way connected with the subject she is studying. What are the interpretative elements of this article? To what extent does this article fall short or meet the criteria for being an interpretative inquiry? Write your answer to these questions with one or two sentences and cite your support by pointing to the page and paragraph where you found that support.

Below is an excellent qualitative study on teaching and learning that is not an interpretative study according to the criteria presented in the preceding chapter. I selected this study to examine because it has a different feel and approach to data collection than the Horowitz (2010) study. Though the study is of high quality, the weakness of the study is that it does not have a well-developed data analysis section.

Learning to learn from benchmark assessment data: How teachers analyze results.
Leslie Nabors Oláh, Nancy R. Lawrence, and Matthew Riggan (2010),
Peabody Journal of Education, 85(2): 226–245.

What is the purpose of the research and what were the findings?
"The purpose of this study is to learn more about the impact of interim assessment on teacher practice" (p. 227). More specifically the study looked at (1) how the teachers analyzed the assessment results, (2) how they planned for instruction based on the results, and (3) how they reported using the results in their teaching (p. 227). The researchers found that teachers developed implicit "thresholds" regarding student performance based on a variety of interconnected factors including students' background, how the items fit into the school curriculum and pace cycle, and whether the specifics of the math content were considered difficult. The authors found that teachers used the benchmark data in a consistent, effective manner and in line with school district expectations. The researchers presented a model of teacher processes for analyzing, interpreting, and acting on benchmark data.

What were the data-collection methods?
The authors interviewed all third and fifth grade teachers in five average-and-above-average-performing elementary schools (a total of 25 teachers) three times during a school year. Additionally the researchers observed one math lesson during the revisit, re-teach, practice, and enrich week. The researchers conducted interviews and gathered observational data three times during the academic year. The interviews occurred within an hour after the classroom observation except for the spring interview that took place two weeks after the observation due to the administration of state tests that followed immediately after the classroom observations (pp. 228–229).

What were the data-analysis methods?
While the authors present a protocol as to how the teachers analyzed the benchmark data collected by the school district there is no discussion of the way they analyzed their data.

Research exercise 4.2: Raising questions

Read the full text of the above article and ask yourself the questions below.

In what ways does this study fulfill or not fulfill the requirements of being an interpretative inquiry?

Examine the full text of this article and find support for, or claims that would challenge my assessment regarding the orientation of the researchers to their subjects, whether the inquiry is "in the middle of things" or whether the researchers see themselves in some way connected with the subject they are studying? What are the interpretative elements of this article? To what extent does this article fall short of being an interpretative inquiry? Write your answer to these questions with one or two sentences and cite your support by pointing to the page and paragraph where you found that support. Also, examine the article closely to see if you can find a comprehensive statement about how the authors conducted their data analysis.

Now let us examine an article that is quantitative and meets the criteria for being an interpretative inquiry. My point is to establish a strong contrast between an article that is clearly positivist and an article that is clearly interpretative. This will help you to sort through the two articles that follow – one mixed method and the other quantitative, both these articles will be within the parameters of interpretative inquiry.

Distance from peers in the group's perceived organizational structure: Relationships to individual characteristics.

A. Michele Lease, Richard M. McFall, and Richard J. Viken (2003),
Journal of Early Adolescence, 23(2): 194–217.

What is the purpose of the research and what were the findings?

The purpose of this research was to uncover young adolescents' implicit perceptions (or social maps) of their peer group. The authors stated that these social maps are not fixed, but undergo revisions as the students and the environment change. The researchers also wanted to find the behavioral characteristics associated with peer-rejection and the relation between these students' behavioral characteristics and their distance from peers within the peer groups' organizational structure. They found peer-group members held convergent perceptions on the organization of the group; in other words, group members saw the internal representation of the group in a similar manner. "The results indicated that the farther a group member was from the origin of their peer group's perceived organizational structure, the more odd, less cool, and less fun to hang around he or she was perceived to be by peers" (p. 207). Students saw learning to fit with peers as a social developmental task. They also saw being perceived as dissimilar as having potential negative connotations.

What were the data-collection methods?
For the purposes of this study, the authors defined "peer group" as the set of same-gender students within a classroom. They collected data on 487 fourth grade students from 26 classrooms. Students were asked to rate pairs of students (similarity judgments) on a 1–7 scale (very different to very alike). The authors asked participants to nominate up to three of their classmates for parts in a play (the parts are not designated). When selecting a person for the part the students in the study were to designate whether the person was "cool," "fun to hang around," had "communication skills," "cooperates," is "inattentive, is "hyperactive or impulsive," a "bully," "shy or anxious," or "excluded." They asked participants to list three of their classmates who they liked most and three classmates that they liked least.

What were the data-analysis methods?
The researchers used badness-of-fit values to determine similarity judgments. The peer group's perceptual organization was compared with the relationship between individuals' social and behavioral characteristics.

Research exercise 4.3: Raising questions

Examine the full text of this article and find support for, or claims that would challenge my assessment regarding the orientation of the researchers to their subjects, whether the inquirers see the students as "in the middle of things" or whether the researchers see themselves in some way connected with the subject they are studying. What are the interpretative elements of this article? To what extent does this article fall short of being an interpretative inquiry? Write your answer to these questions with one or two sentences and cite your support by pointing to the page and paragraph where that support is found.

A mixed method study that fits within the interpretative framework is our next illustration. For this example, I turn to a study conducted with a group of undergraduate students (Morehouse *et al.* 2009). This study uses both qualitative and quantitative measures to gain a close perspective on the teaching/learning process in a semester long small group tutoring program conducted by students with other students.

A microgenetic study of the tutoring process: Learning center research.
Richard E. Morehouse, Aleksey Sakharuk, Samantha Merry,
Violeta Kadieva, Mallory Nesberg (2009),
The Journal of Pedagogical Research and Scholarship, 1(2): 13–25.

What is the purpose of the research and what were the findings?
The purpose of this inquiry was to gain a fine-grained picture of the session-by-session experience of tutors and students over the course of a semester. The inquiry further looked to find links between student scores on ASSIST (Centre for Research on

Learning and Instruction 2006) and theories of intelligence scales (Dweck 1999). ASSIST scores provide a measure of students' approach to study; a student has either a surface approach to learning or a deep approach to learning. Dweck's measure provides a score that places students into either an incremental or entity view of intelligence. A person with an incremental view sees intelligence as improvable by effort, while an entity score indicates that the person sees intelligence as a fixed commodity.

This study also sought to find a relationship between these scores and student performance as measured by course grade. The qualitative results yielded three propositions. First, tutors organized and taught their session based on their own self-theory of intelligence by using different levels of understanding. Second, tutors' self-theories of intelligence affected the overall approach to study. Third, based on the self-theory of intelligence, the two tutoring sessions differed with regard to the frequency and types of tutor praise as well as the number and quality of student-initiated questions.

The quantitative part of this inquiry found several trends but no changes that were statistically significant. First, there was a significant increase in the surface approach to the study score of the tutored students by the tutor with an entity score on the Dweck's self-theory of intelligence scale. There was a non-statistically significant correlation in the predicted direction between students with an incremental orientation toward intelligence (Dweck 1999) and students with a deep approach to study (Centre for Research on Learning and Instruction 2006). Another trend was that students with the highest scores on surface learning had the lowest course grades. Finally, grades for incremental students were higher than grades for entity students but the difference was not statistically significant.

What were the data-collection methods?
The authors video-recorded and transcribed all tutoring sessions. The researchers administered the ASSIST assessment (Centre for Research on Learning and Instruction 2006) and Dweck's theories of intelligence (1999) instruments to all students and tutors before the tutoring session began.

What were the data-analysis methods?
The members of the research team transcribed the videos verbatim. The team transcribed the video recording a second time to ensure accuracy and to familiarize the researchers with the sessions. The transcripts were then broken into units of meaning, and categorized using the constant comparison method. The research team placed the units into categories using this method. Later, the researchers utilized a second data analysis approach. The categories of describing, relating, explaining, and conceiving from Entwistle's model (Entwistle 2000: 5) were used to redistribute the units of meaning. Finally, Dweck's work on types of praise provided an additional tool to explore the tutors' use of either praise for ability or praise for effort.

The research team used correlation measures and t-test to compare scores on ASSIST and theories of intelligence and between ASSIST scores and course grades, as well as between theories of intelligence scores and course grades.

Research exercise 4.4: Raising questions

Following the protocol used in this chapter for examining research exercises, read carefully the full text of this article and find support for, or claims that would challenge my assessment regarding the orientation of the researchers to their subjects, whether the inquirers see the students as "in the middle of things" or whether the researchers see themselves in some way connected with the subject they are studying. What are the interpretative elements of this article? To what extent does this article fall short of being an interpretative inquiry? Write your answer to these questions with one or two sentences and cite your support by pointing to the page and paragraph where that support is found.

Summary

I selected each of the above articles to illustrate a fit or lack of fit with the interpretative stance toward research. Being able to recognize what an interpretative inquiry article or evaluation project looks like is important not only for the construction of your own projects but also during the review of the literature process. While one does not need to cite only inquiries that are within the interpretative framework in the review of the literature, it is helpful to be able to recognize the framework within which the research is conducted as the results are colored by the research framework. A careful study of other interpretative inquiries will provide clues as how you might proceed with your own project. Examine the non-interpretative studies you include in your research in the light of their ontology and their epistemology. Seen through the lens of ontology and epistemology these studies can contribute to our greater understanding of the phenomena under investigation. Without some sense of how a variety of studies fit together you may not be able to get a good picture of the phenomena and doing a critical review of the literature becomes challenging. The points will be further developed in Chapters 5 and 9.

Part 11

From ideas to publication

Chapter 5

Transition

Key terms to understand in the practice of interpretative inquiry

Many of the key terms important to interpretative inquiry are more closely related to terms and concepts found in qualitative inquiry than they are to terms in quantitative research and evaluation. These qualitative-like terms have a somewhat different valence when used in an interpretative inquiry: thus there is a corresponding modification in the labeling and definition of these terms. Readers familiar with qualitative research will recognize the origins of these concepts; therefore, the reader should not only pay attention to the similarities but also to the differences. Interpretative inquiry projects, like many qualitative projects, are exploratory and theory driven, using situational and holistic analysis of complex, dynamic, and experiential phenomena. These projects seek to understand meaning from the perspective of the participants. They may also analyze of aesthetic dimensions of experience. Most interpretative projects focus on relational analysis and reflexivity (Camic *et al.* 2003).

> What distinguishes an interpretative approach is not what methods it uses – qualitative, textual data, for example, or quantitative analysis; rather, the distinction lies in considering the ontological and epistemological standpoint the researcher brings to bear in his or her social inquiry.
>
> (Hesse-Biber 2010: 104)

As discussed extensively in the previous chapters, interpretative inquiry is about trying to capture people's action and efforts to make meaning in a lived context. The interpretative inquiry begins with the Gestalt, that big picture, and then looks at the pieces to understand the whole more clearly. This whole-part back and forth examination of the lived experience is the essence of the interpretative process.

I will first address the key terms and provide their definitions before proceeding to articulate the way interpretative inquiry addresses the issues presented above. The key terms I define and provide examples for are human instruments, evolving design, situated exploration, relational engagement, deep probing, and contextual analysis.

Human instruments

The concept of "human instruments" is defined as a set of approaches to understanding the phenomena under investigation by using data-gathering tools that reflect the complex and integrated relationships that underlie our ability to understand other human interactions. The term is derived from what Lincoln and Guba (1985) call "human-as-instrument." They argue that human behavior is too complex to be measured by any other instrument than another human being. I have two concerns with that position. First, Lincoln and Guba's position implies that it is possible for one human being to fully understand another human being. While they do not go that far, their writing leads in that direction. The other point, and this Lincoln and Guba make directly, is that non-human instruments cannot adequately represent important human experiences.

I will begin with the implied statement by Lincoln and Guba (1985) that it is possible for one human being to fully or near fully understand another human being. Even as a goal, this concept belies the situational nature of interpretative inquiry and what Lincoln and Guba call naturalistic inquiry. The best we can hope for is a rich understanding of persons in specific relationships in a specific environment. While this may seem like a small point, it has important implications in the way we conduct, analyze, and write-up our findings.

The second point, that nothing other than a human being is capable of capturing contextual human experiences, is equally important in understanding interpretative inquiry. Michael Westerman and Edward Steen (2009), in an article on conflict and defensive behavior, present a creative way to capture some important elements of human interaction within a given context. The Westerman and Steen article provides but one example. At the core of their approach is using quantifiable data to support inquiry about persons in a relational context. The collection of this data and the data reduction that follows needs to remain sensitive to the integration of the people and situations under investigation. The goal of human instruments is to seek to reveal the structure of a given experience within a specific context and with awareness of the limits of generalization.

Human instruments include not only scenarios like the ones developed by Westerman and Steen (2009) in order to learn more about defensive behaviors in context, but also such traditional human instruments as open-ended and semi-structured interview schedules, document analysis, progress assessments, and various observation techniques. What one needs to pay attention to is the establishment and maintenance of a relational-contextual orientation that values the meaning-making capacity of the participants in the inquiry project.

One of the reasons that interpretative inquiry uses the tool of human instruments has to do with causation. Aristotle articulated four forms of causality – formal (quality or essence), final (end state or goal), material (physical make-up), and efficient (effects of prior events, i.e. mechanical causes). Traditional inquiry tends to focus exclusively on the effect of prior events, or cause and effect as we have written earlier in Chapters 1 and 2 (McGrath and Johnson 2003: 36). Final causes are what concern me here.

Understanding people's goals is essential to understanding the actions of others in relationships. However, understanding goals is not an important part of traditional positivist oriented inquiry. This is partially because goals are not easy to capture using traditional quantitative measures. Humans-as-instruments and humanly constructed instruments have the potential to capture human goals, even when these goals are somewhat transient.

Research exercise 5.1: Human instruments

Human instruments need to understand the role of goals as they relate to the participants' actions. Yet much research ignores or does not even look at the role that personal beliefs, goals, or desires play in understanding how they come to engage in a particular activity, or why they succeed or fail at a particular activity.

   Albert Bandura (1997) is one of the researchers who takes people's goals and desires seriously. He argues that challenging goals engender greater effort than easily attained goals; however, some people reject goals that are too challenging. As a person interested in the importance of individual goals, how would you go about finding out which goals are challenging, which are too easy, and which are too challenging?

- What questions would you asked the students?
- How would you go about helping students identify their personal goals?
- What patterns would you seek to find in the students' work as they strived to complete the assigned tasks?

While understanding goals or final causes are not the only areas that a human instrument needs to address, goals influence human activities in important ways and should not be ignored by interpretative inquirers.

> Mental states, such as beliefs, desires, emotions intentions, and goals comprise a primary causal mechanism for human actions. In particular, because goals and intentions organize and motivate actions, reasoning about the goals underlying others' actions is central to social understanding.
>
> (Pillow *et al.* 2008: 472)

Evolving design

Evolving design is a research plan that establishes and defends the choice of:

1 inquiry question(s),
2 data collection methods, and
3 approaches to data analysis while allowing for some modification as new information is gathered and tentatively analyzed.

All three of the design elements may change, although the changes are likely to be modifications of a well thought-out plan.

Inquiry questions

An interpretative inquiry shares the following characteristics with a qualitative study: it is likely to be conducted in a messy situation. Multiple variables are used to explore the specific characteristics of the situation. The design is open-ended and flexible. It will include social interaction directed toward developing a profile that is constructed and designed by the researcher but modified through engagement with participants in a co-creative approach (Schoenfeld 2009). Qualitative researchers label the way they approach a research design as emergent. These researchers focus their attention primarily on the *emergent* part of emergent design. In an interpretative inquiry, the researchers and evaluators need to pay equal amounts of attention to the design and the emergent.

In order to balance attention to both the changing or emergent elements of the project and the design elements of the project, I have called this phase of project development *evolving design*. In developing an interpretative study, the conceptualization of the study is of paramount importance. This conceptualization begins with the framing of the inquiry question. The questions that one develops for an interpretative inquiry should be sensitive to the complex relationships between the inquirer and the participant in their specific situations. This move is evolving in two ways. First it moves away from a static, proof-oriented, strictly experimental model often conducted in a lab, toward a situational, discovery, and explanatory study in a more natural setting. Next, it allows for some modification and change in the details of the design as the project unfolds. However, the design is also anchored in a specific question or set of questions. Therefore, I am reluctant to call this an emergent design, as the initial questions are likely to be more specifically defined than an open-ended focus of inquiry (see Maykut and Morehouse 1994, or Lincoln and Guba 1985).

An evolving design is one that is anchored in a specific question with a defined approach to data collection and analysis but is open to modification and revision as new information and data are collected and analyzed. This evolution may occur over the course of several pilot studies, or it may occur in phases of a single study. It may also occur in either the data collection or data analysis phases

Methods of data collection

How do we catch ongoing action by agents who are seeking meaning? Most qualitative data meets these criteria. Audio and video recording of classroom activities, therapy sessions, work meetings, and planning sessions are specific examples of interpretative data. Interviews that in an open-ended manner focus on the meaning of people's actions and ideas are also good examples of interpretative data. I would place the work of Mary Belenky and colleagues (1984) in the category of interpretative inquiry data collection. The challenge is how to collect quantitative data within the interpretative framework.

Following Michael Westerman (2006), I take an interpretative stand for using a hermeneutic perspective on quantitative data. Westerman argues that operationally defined behavioral codes are interpretative (Westerman 2006: 191). Self-reports are also interpretative (p. 192). In an imaginative study, Michael Westerman and Edward Steen (2009) use relational theories of defense and discourse analysis to capture responses that are interactive and agentic in an ongoing, open-ended scenario. By audio recording the role-plays, the researchers are able to capture how individuals respond within a relational dyad to conflict and non-conflict scenarios. "This was determined by measuring to what extent the participant's unscripted contributions to the exchange were coordinating or noncoordinating, that is, the extent to which they were characterized by discourse breaches" (Westerman and Steen 2009: 338). A discourse breach occurs when a person changes the direction of the conversation in order to avoid the consequences of maintaining the discourse. The discourse breaches were counted and compared under conflict and non-conflict situations.

Westerman and Steen (2009) provide an insight into how one can examine process within relationships while collecting quantitative data. Their work is consistent with others who work in discourse analysis. Rom Harré's work on positioning theory is another example (see Harré, and van Langenhove 1999). Positioning, according to Davies and Harré (1999), is defined as the discursive process whereby selves are located in conversation within a jointly produced story line (Spreckels 2008).

Methods of data analysis

The question of data analysis has several layers. The first question relates to the types of data to be collected and is addressed above. Once you have collected the data the next question is how ought the data be analyzed? The analysis of qualitative data is relatively straightforward.

Qualitative data analysis

Any of the typical qualitative data analysis methods are workable, though approaches that use pre-established codes are suspect. Discourse analysis (Davies and Harré 1990; Potter 2003) phenomenological analysis including phenomenography (Marton 1986), the constant comparative method (Glaser and Strauss 1967; Maykut and Morehouse 1994; Henwood and Pidgeon 2003), narrative analysis (Murray 2003), or participatory action research (Fine and Torre 2004). Many of these approaches to qualitative data analysis will be discussed in some detail in Chapter 8.

Quantitative data analysis

While I have made the case for an interpretative orientation to quantitative data analysis, I have yet to provide specific reasons for interpretative quantitative data analysis. Westerman asks what I think is a key question regarding the use of quantitative data in interpretative studies. "Why should we use quantitative methods instead of or in addition to qualitative methods when the latter are expressly interpretative and have a great deal to offer?" (Westerman 2006: 195). Two reasons from Westerman's argument stand out for me. First, quantitative measures are a good method for comparing two groups on some specific measure. Second, quantitative measures make specific meaning concrete. These and other points regarding quantitative measures and data analysis will be explored in Chapter 8.

Quantitative/qualitative data analysis

The key point here is not the inclusion of qualitative and quantitative measures in the same study, but rather how these methods of data collection and analysis are combined. Steven Yanchar and David Williams (2006) provide some important guidelines for combining data from quantitative and qualitative sources. They argue that inquirers need to be sensitive to context. Inquirers also need to use creativity when constructing theory, formulating questions, and solving problems. Importantly, inquirers should be informed by some theoretical and historical sense of the topic of interest and what appears to be the most defensible procedure answering the question and solving the problem (Yanchar and Williams 2006: 9). Coherence is another important ingredient if one is going to effectively combine quantitative and qualitative data. Therefore, "questions, methods, practices, and interpretations should fit strategically within some larger purpose" (Yanchar and Williams 2006: 9) and should not be contradictory or self-refuting. Finally, critical reflection is an important element needed to integrate qualitative and quantitative data. This means that the inquirers need to see their assumptions that frame their interpretative inquiry as fallible, alterable, and in need of critical examination (ibid.).

Relational engagement

Relational engagement extends the idea of human instruments from the examination of the research question to include the review of the literature, the selection of the population, and the relationship with the stakeholders. Relational engagement is defined as the effort to bring an integrated situational and historic perspective to the overall orientation of the project. Maintaining an awareness of the person and the situation being studied is essential if one is to be relationally engaged. Stated somewhat differently, it means not losing sight of the lived experiences of the study participants who are engaged in intercourse with specific persons, environments, and cultures. An example of relational engagement is a study conducted by Janet Spreckels (2008) entitled "Identity negotiation in small stories among German adolescent girls." The author uses positioning analysis, identities-in-interaction, and membership categories to study the "small stories" of girls who are negotiating and constructing group and gender identities. A subsection of the paper entitled "The girls: a 'community of practice'" captures the participants' efforts at negotiating identities and building relationships. Spreckels writes, "Through their regular gatherings, members of a CoP (Community of Practice) developed shared values, norms and communication practices. These common resources are the result of an extended period of mutual interaction" (2008: 399).

Deep probing

Deep probing is an effort to understand the research question by using approaches that get beyond the surface meanings in order to see the situation within an ongoing process and locate the connections of people, ideas, and actions within specific spaces and times. This is done by conducting in-depth interviews, engaging in extended observations, collecting documents over an extended period of time, and by triangulating several sources of data. An example of this can be found in Gallucci et al.'s (2010) article on instructional coaching. Examining in detail a single case from a four-year longitudinal study involving coaches in three school districts:

> We analysed the experiences of one coach (called Dan in this article) because he was the focal coach in one middle school research site and we had a robust account of his experiences from December 2006 through February 2008. The fact that we had 14 months of observational data about his learning and that he was articulate about the meaning of these experiences made his case an instrumental one (Stake 1995) for examining the broader problem of how coaches learn to do their work. The deep analysis of a single case allowed rich detail and nuance that might have been lost if we had generalized across multiple or comparative cases. Our purpose was to develop hypotheses based on Dan's in-depth case that would lead to future research regarding coaches' learning.
>
> (Gallucci et al. 2010: 928)

This example focuses on how a single case may be used to accomplish deep probing. However, deep probing may also occur through the use of multiple cases using both qualitative and quantitative data collection methods.

Contextual analysis

Contextual analysis includes a set of data analysis tools that maintains the interpretative elements of the collected data. This means that all data whether qualitative or quantitative needs to be relational, contextual, about agents seeking and making meaning, and within historic and relational patterns. Westerman and Stern's 2007 and 2009 articles on interpersonal defense provide examples of contextual analysis. These authors provide a theoretical perspective on what they call a participatory account of psychological phenomena. While what I am calling contextual analysis is not exactly the same as a participatory account, a participatory account is sensitive to the same ways of looking at understanding persons in action. Westerman and Steen state,

> We call models of this type participant accounts to signify two things: (1) that the subject of such an account is a participant in meaningful practices, and (2) that the psychologist developing the account also is participating in the world of practical activities.
>
> (2007: 330)

One of the key elements of this approach is that understanding an individual's or group's behavior depends on the role they play in contexts of practical activities (ibid.: 331). Notably, Westerman and Steen argue that in order to properly understand an individual's behavior one must see that behavior as "dovetailing" with the behavior of others (ibid.: 332). Perhaps even more important for the contextual analysis of human interaction is an awareness that psychological phenomena always rest on our prior familiarity with what Wittgenstein called "forms of life" (ibid.: 335). "Because our understanding rests upon – rather than fully explicates – our prior involvement in practice, it is irreducibly interpretative and remains incomplete, rather than the crystalline, fully explicit kind of knowledge most psychologists aspire to attain" (ibid: 335).

Summary

With a working understanding of some of the key terms and concepts that relate to interpretative inquiry, you are now ready to begin your research project. The next chapter will walk you through the process of coming up with and organizing some ideas, to launching an interpretative inquiry project. You may find it helpful to occasionally look back at some of the earlier chapters in order to stay grounded in the philosophical orientation of interpretative inquiry; however, you know enough to move forward with your project.

Chapter 6

Where do ideas come from?

Developing ideas for inquiry projects

This chapter continues the practical problems phase of developing a researchable interpretative project. Conducting an inquiry project of any size may at first appear to be a daunting task. To make that process manageable, I will provide a step-by-step outline designed to move from a research idea to a written statement of research purpose (defining the problem) to a researchable question to a conceptual plan for a study. While there are challenges to beginning an inquiry project, even a person new to interpretative inquiry has the assets needed to conceptualize, initiate, and complete a project. Assessing the assets needed to conduct an inquiry project, along with breaking the task down into smaller steps, will help to ensure that your project can be completed.

The first stage of any research project is the planning phase. Even the planning stage can appear overwhelming if one looks only at the big picture. I will, therefore, break the process down into to the following steps:

1   coming up with ideas for an inquiry project,
2   translating those ideas into a researchable interpretative question, and
3   conceptualizing and writing an interpretative inquiry proposal.

Each of these three steps will be further broken down into smaller steps.

Coming up with ideas has two main sources: wide and critical reading, and observation. Marginal notes taken from your reading and the observations recorded in the inquirer's notebook will be used in this phase. The section on how one translates ideas into researchable questions is parsed into the following categories: (1) what makes an idea researchable? and (2) transforming researchable ideas into interpretative questions. The thinking tools of brainstorming and concept maps will be used to move ideas gained from reading and observation to researchable questions for inquiry. Conceptualizing an interpretative inquiry proposal is presented as a single section.

Coming up with ideas for an inquiry project

If you have ever scratched your head and said, "I wonder …" you have an idea that is potentially researchable. Researchable ideas come from anywhere and everywhere. Ideas for projects are all around us, but how to access these ideas is sometimes problematic. As Louis Pasteur once said "discovery favors the prepared mind." This is also true for discovering good inquiry questions. Two ways to build up your catalog of potential research ideas are reading and observation. I begin with reading.

Wide and critical reading

The more you read research the more ideas you will have to work with. Reading research articles opens the mind to possibilities in a general way as well as to specific ideas. As you read, you see what and how other researchers think, what interests them, and how they organize their thoughts on paper. Research articles also provide a specific place to look for new ideas. Most research articles will end with a discussion section that includes the author(s)' suggestions for further research.

These suggestions are invitations for you to make a leap into your own project. It can also be seen as an invitation to contact the author(s) of the project to ask a question about her or his project or sharpen an idea for research that you have. Most often researchers will be flattered that you are interested in their projects and they may give you a hand or a steer towards your own work.

Wide reading of research articles also allows the possibility of seeing connections between different research projects that the authors themselves may not have seen. One advantage that I mentioned earlier is that new researchers are not stuck in a research trench, if you will. In other words, as a new researcher, you may have more eclectic reading habits than researchers who have been working in the field for a long time. On the negative end of the spectrum, eclectic reading may sometimes lead the inquirer far afield from a researchable topic; however, it may also lead to juxtaposing ideas that would not have occurred to veteran researchers.

In addition to reading widely, critical reading of research projects is also helpful (Yudkin 2006). By critical reading I mean careful reading, often including marginal notes or other methods for commenting on the article as you read it. By taking notes while reading, one gains a perspective on both the content of the article and the processes of writing. Each section of an article may have something that contributes to the generation of ideas. The author's look at previous research, or the way she puts that research together in some sort of coherent whole, may give you a new insight. The way the author chooses to collect or analyze her data may spark an idea. Previous marginal notes may also connect to what you are currently reading.

Some of the marginal notes should find their way into the inquirer's notebook. This notebook was started as a part of a research exercise in Chapter 1. If you have not been actively using it up until now, it's time to take some of your marginal notes for the several articles you read as a part of the research exercises and put them into your notebook. If you have not been using your researcher's notebook, it's time to start. A way to transfer this information is to summarize the key ideas (both methods and findings) in a short paragraph. Some people like to place these notes on index cards. I prefer to place the articles in a folder on my computer. This will allow for easy access as you begin to use the notebook more actively.

Making a chart that summarizes the articles you have read is also an effective way to both keep track of your reading as well as a vehicle for organizing your research reading. You may wish to summarize your research articles in a chart like Table 6.1.

Table 6.1 Article summaries.

Full reference for the article including title, date, authors, and where published	Hypothesis or aims of the inquiry	Key findings	Independent variables	Dependent variables	Suggestions for further research

You can organize your observations for your researcher's notebook in a similar manner. Here is one possible way to organize your observational notes. Ask yourself the following questions: What is it about the topic that interested me? Is it the problem being addressed? Is it the way the researcher conceptualized the problem? Is it how the problem is related to other things that interest me?

After examining your marginal notes and your entries in your notebook, conduct a mental survey of your recent and long-term reading habits. Which scholars in your field or related fields do you find yourself returning to? Is there a scholar whose work you keep reading even though it is not directly connected with your day-to-day reading requirements? Is there a pattern in the topics in your notebook or notes from your reading that continues to attract your attention? The answers to these questions provide a strong indication of the areas of research and perhaps the style of research that you are drawn to. Mine these sources for research topics. If you have already done some research, look back on your past writing, thinking, and research projects, and ask what remains to be done. What ideas surface as you reflect on your past learning and involvement?

Research exercise 6.1: Using the inquirer's notebook

Go back to the research notebook that you began in Research Exercise 1.1, or if you have not been actively keeping up your notebook, reflect back on the questions raised above. Read what you have in your notebook and based on what you find, list three to five ideas that relate to research. These do not necessarily need to be researchable questions, just ideas. Do any of the ideas you listed continue to spark your interest? Can you modify a less interesting idea so that it more closely fits your current interests? How much do you know about the issue? Would you like to know more about one of the specific issues found in your notebook? What about this idea draws you into wanting to study it more thoroughly? Your answers to these questions may be the beginning of your interpretative inquiry project.

Observation

Observations come in many different forms. Not all observations are conducted formally and systematically. If fact, most of our lives are spent in informal observation – it's called living. These informal observations, along with more systematic ones, are a rich source of ideas for research. Consistent with an interpretative orientation, it is important to examine one's situated and lived experiences. I recommend looking in three directions to flush out ideas for an inquiry project: look back, look ahead, and look around.

To examine the first of the three directions, what does it mean to look back? It means looking at one's own experiences, one's own reading, and one's own research. Looking back has been the major focus of the Research Exercise 6.1. To extend this look backwards the following questions may be helpful. Are there issues, concerns or questions that you would explore if you only had the time? Are there unanswered, maybe even unasked, questions that arise out from that backwards glance? Are there researchers and theorists that you like to read whenever you have a bit of time? Do you find yourself chatting with friends and colleagues about a social or educational problem? An affirmative answer to any of these questions is an indication that you may have found a fruitful topic for inquiry.

What does looking around mean? Perhaps an example of someone looking around will help. Hans Eysenck, while working in a psychological clinic during World War II, looked around and wondered if psychoanalytic therapy was an effective way for people to address personal problems or did many people get better or solve their psychological problems by themselves over time? His controversial study (Hunt 1993: 595–596) led to systematic research and helped to launch his career. Eysenck's research does not fit the interpretative inquiry framework, but it is a good example of how a question based on an informal observation may lead to a researchable topic.

Another way of looking around is to ask: What are my colleagues doing? What are the professional concerns that are popping up in the literature? What projects need to be addressed? Looking for what needs to be done is an important generic strategy. Someone recently argued that new university graduates should enter into their careers by asking where the work is rather that where the jobs are. He was encouraging new professionals to look to the problems that confront the larger world today. Martin Seligman's presidential address (1998) presents a similar sentiment. That sentiment might also guide inquiry questions.

Finally, look ahead. What project would you like to be involved with but have been, up until now, unwilling to address? Perhaps there is a small part of that big project that you can begin to explore in a somewhat systematic manner. What other ideas are related to that project? Use these questions and thought experiments (*Gedankenexperiment*) to begin this research exercise.

Notes from your reading, as well as systematic and casual observations, may find their way into a research notebook. A researcher's notebook is a handy tool to keep by your side. It's a place to keep unkempt thoughts, beginnings of ideas, rewrites of earlier ideas, and project ideas as they begin to form in your mind. Think of a researcher's notebook as a petri dish where things germinate. What germinates will not always be a good idea but, as with brainstorming, many ideas may lead to one or two good ideas.

Brainstorming research ideas

Another approach to accessing ideas for research is through brainstorming. Brainstorming may be most helpful when working with a small team of researchers. It allows several people to get their ideas out in the open in a non-threatening way and allows people with different ideas to find, and build on, mutual interests.

Research exercise 6.2: Developing research ideas through a group brainstorming activity

A brainstorming activity is merely a listing of ideas about a topic without censoring them while you are in the process of listing. The point is that sometimes good ideas are likely to come late in the process, that is, ordinary, typical ideas come first while more unique, interesting ideas may come later in the list. You are now asked to brainstorm a response to what you see as you look forward, backwards, and around. Working in a group, use a big piece of paper or a black- or whiteboard or computer-projected images to collect the group's thought. One of the important ideas to remember is that "piggy-backing," that is, building on the ideas of your colleagues is not only okay, it is recommended. Closely related to "piggy-backing" is the point that no idea is a bad idea – it's just an idea – it can be corrected, modified, or disposed of later. For now it is an idea and it goes up on the big paper or board.

Begin with the direction (back, forward, or around) that initially appears most fruitful. List at least 15 uncensored statements. But don't stop there if ideas are flowing. Do not be concerned if these statements are not in the form of a question. That is a later step. The point here is to generate potential ideas for a researchable topic.

Now pick the next direction (back, forward, or around) and do the same thing. Next pick the remaining direction and again list at least 15 items that come to mind. You now have at least 30 potential ideas. Review your comments for each of the directions. Look for patterns in your statements or ideas. If there are, group them together. With that grouping before you, write a tentative research question. This is tentative, as we will later reframe that question as an interpretative question.

You may also do a similar process working alone. If you are working alone take out a blank sheet of paper and label it brainstorming. Next place the three direction words on the top of the page in columns. Draw lines to separate the columns. The rest of the activity unfolds similarly to the group activity.

Brainstorming is a tool, but does not substitute for quiet rumination, thoughtful reflection, or kicking around ideas with colleague. As a tool it can be helpful when one gets stuck or as a way to uncover ideas that you may not have noticed with the usual approaches to generating ideas. There is no substitute for systematic and careful reading supplemented by extensive research notes with or without file cards.

Making ideas public: concept-maps and inquiry questions

The next step is to make your ideas for inquiry public as you place them within a larger context. What is important is to get the ideas onto paper, or a whiteboard, or a computer screen. My experience is that while my own ideas may seem rich, complex, and interesting as I ruminate about them in the privacy of my own thinking, when I begin to put them on paper (figuratively or literally), my ideas often appear less clear and more vague. This does not mean that they were or are bad ideas; it is descriptive of how my mind works. By making them public, that is, external to myself and accessible to others, I usually can make my ideas clearer. Making a concept map is one way to make one's ideas clearer.

A concept-map is one way of taking a snapshot of one's current thinking before the project begins. It helps to make clearer what both individuals and the group of researchers are thinking about the project's inquiry question. A concept-map begins by placing a key concept in the middle of the page and then connecting that concept with related ideas – ideas that extend, define, limit, or clarify the idea in the center of the page. These maps can be simple or complex with one and two way arrows (representing the direction of influence), solid and dotted lines (indicating overt or covert influences or strong or weak influences) or circles, rectangles, and triangles (representing nouns, verbs, or modifiers). The maps are only limited by one's imagination. These maps are helpful in getting some of your ideas clearer and allowing you to see the relationships among and between ideas. They can also be helpful in explaining your ideas to colleagues and fellow students as you work to select a joint research project.

Figure 6.1 is a generic concept/mind-map. I chose to present a generic one in order to illustrate the various elements without the distraction of trying to figure out how one might apply this to a new project.

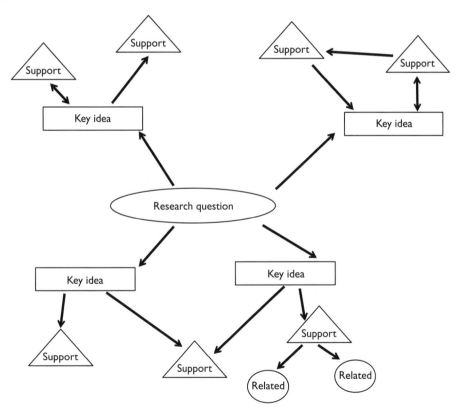

Figure 6.1 Generic concept/mind-map.

In a student/faculty inquiry project, maps similar to this one were used to develop an interview protocol as well as in the creation and selection of paper and pencil instruments used in the study. This model is presented merely to illustrate what a concept map might look like. The point is that these concept-maps provide an early look at what an individual or group thinks about the topic before beginning to look at it in more detail and may be used as one tool for keeping important elements of the conceptual frame of your project in the foreground.

Research activity 6.3: Making a concept map

With your brainstorming list in front of you, begin the process of sifting through the ideas to see which ideas might be worth pursuing. Now is the time to correct, modify, or dispose of any of the ideas you see fit. Of the worthwhile ideas that are left, choose two ideas that most interest you or the group from which to make mind-maps. Again, a mind-map is your attempt to show connections to a main idea. This process allows for the contextualization of your topic.

These mind-maps now become working documents from which to create research questions and further define your research goals. These mind-maps are the beginning thoughts for your research or evaluation project.

As the next section explores other ways of finding ideas for inquiry topics, it is important to keep in mind that none of the topics developed thus far will be your final research project. The purpose of this exercise is primarily to provide a vehicle for "unsticking" your thoughts. Your head may already be overflowing with ideas. If that's the case, save these ideas for a later date.

Formulating and asking interpretative questions

Does it matter the language we use to formulate our inquiry? While it may not be essential that specific, consistent language be used when writing our inquiry questions, it helps. Labels matter. A hypothesis is a hunch that the researcher is attempting to prove or disprove; therefore, it is likely to position the project on the positivist end of the naturalist paradigm. A focus of inquiry is a qualitative inquiry term that implies a more-or-less open-ended and contextual inquiry; thus, the project is likely positioned at the naturalist end of the paradigm.

I have chosen to use the words "interpretative questions" for an interpretative inquiry as it keeps the focus open-ended and contextual without designating it as qualitative or quantitative. Interpretative questions, as has been emphasized in this work, also bring to mind agency, action, and meaning-making. It is important to note that some researchers working within an interpretative framework use the term "hypothesis." If a project has an authentic interpretative orientation it will indicate that the focus is on agency, action, and meaning-making. Westerman and colleagues, in an examination of children's beliefs about defensive interpersonal behavior, state one of their hypotheses that provides just such a focus.

We hypothesized that children understand that defensive behavior plays a functional role in interpersonal interaction, in particular, that (1) they understand that it feeds forward to affect interaction events by reducing the likelihood that fears and wished-for short-term outcomes will occur.

(Westerman *et al*. 2007: 295)

In order to ask interpretative questions, I begin with some background on focus of inquiry versus hypothesis. A qualitative study typically begins with determining the focus of inquiry. A focus of inquiry implies an open-ended investigation; a discovery is the intended outcome. A hypothesis, on the other hand, is an educated guess regarding a prediction. A hypothesis is about cause and effect. An interpretative question is situated someplace between a focus of inquiry and a hypothesis.

An interpretative question, like a focus of inquiry, may lead to a discovery. However, an interpretative question sometimes has a clear idea of what is to be found. What a focus of inquiry and an interpretative question share is an interest in context, an effort to understand relationships, and a focus on how the participants create and understand the meaning of their actions. There is a larger difference between a hypothesis and an inquiry question than there is between an inquiry question and a focus of inquiry. Both the inquiry question and the focus of inquiry address issues of what and how, rather than issues of proof. What is central to both inquiry questions and a focus of inquiry is a convergence on persons in specific situations involving actors and meaning-seekers.

A hypothesis, on the other hand, is a statement about the proof or disproof of something. A hypothesis is usually a part of an experimental or quasi-experimental study. A hypothesis directs the researcher to establish a design that will confirm or disconfirm a particular premise. An interpretative question, on the other hand, is defined as a question about an ongoing process that focuses on what is occurring and how it happens. An interpretative question focuses on the meaning of human interaction in specific situations. While an interpretative study may use quantitative, qualitative, or mixed methods of data collection, its focus is on understanding the "what" and "how" of the issue from multiple perspectives.

Asking interpretative questions

Now that you have some ideas together and have sorted out some key differences between focus of inquiry, hypothesis, and interpretative questions, asking a working research question is the next step. A working inquiry question is a first draft, that is, it is unlikely to be fully formed and well stated. Think of the first version of the research questions much like the first draft of a paper; it's a good start but the final question will be considerably changed.

That's not to say that asking good inquiry questions is an overly difficult task, it is only to emphasize that asking questions is as much process as product. As you pen your first interpretative question, you are setting the agenda for your review of the literature, your data collection, and your data analysis. Drawing on your mind-maps and your marginal notes from your earlier reading, you have the beginning of your research question.

An inquiry question may begin with either a broad all-encompassing or a narrowly focused one. The breadth and depth of your first question is not as important as it is to begin by getting something down on the page. A blank page is the enemy of most writers and researchers. Even if you are embarking on an evaluation project, getting an evaluation question or questions down on paper or up on a white- or blackboard, or on your computer, will get you started.

Your study may have one or more questions that you intend to address in this project. Each of the questions should be related, perhaps integrated or nested. Integrated questions are linked in a more-or-less linear manner with the answer to one question leading to the asking and answering of the next question, while with nested questions each question is contained within a larger question. This may be a small difference so allow me to illustrate what I mean. Here is an example of an integrated set of questions. "How do students' perceptions of school environment in seventh grade affect their school participation, school identification, and use of self- regulation strategies in eighth grade?" (Wang and Holcombe 2010). The research question is in fact three questions that are integrated, that is, each question contributes to a partial answer to a bigger question. The bigger question, the nested question from the same article is, "How do these three types of engagement affect their academic achievement in eighth grade?" (ibid.).

Research exercise 6.4: Writing a researchable question

Choose one of the ideas from your brainstorming activities or perhaps the question that is implicit in your mind-map. If you are working in a small group combine the list on a public space (blackboard, white board, big paper or on a screen using your computer and a projector (using a computer for this process can be a helpful way of keeping track of your work as you move from one step to the next)).

Ask: what more about this topic would I like to know? It is helpful to ask your question by using the specific stem: I would like to know more about …. Using this stem lessens the likelihood of phrasing the question as a hypothesis. This phrasing helps to move the question away from a proof-oriented question and toward a "what" and "how" oriented question. By focusing on what and how questions, we are on the naturalists' side of the continuum.

Now ask: what are the interpretative elements in this topic? In what way does the agency of the participants manifest itself? How is this topic embedded in ongoing interactions between and among individuals and/or groups? Is it possible to access the participants meaning-making processes? An affirmative answer to these questions will determine if you have an interpretative question.

Write a first draft of your interpretative question. It is sometimes helpful to put your question aside for an hour or a day and then go back to it with a fresh pair of eyes. Reflect on some of the studies reviewed so far and compare the approach to a research question taken by those authors with your research question. Now rewrite your research question. This is a tentative commitment to begin your project.

An old saying states that to ask a question of a problem is to have half the answer. If that saying holds true, you are well on your way to writing a researchable proposal.

Ideas and evaluation projects

Why worry about getting ideas for evaluation projects? Aren't evaluation questions already settled, either by the granting agency, the group commissioning the evaluation, or some outside agency that has asked you to conduct the evaluation? Sometimes these questions are somewhat settled and what is needed is to figure out a more specific evaluation question.

Other times there is only a vague sense that the framers of the project only want to know whether or not the program successfully met its goals. The first step therefore is to determine the state of the evaluation project.

The project goals are therefore the place to begin. Are the project goals end-states that require a yes or no statement regarding whether or not the goal has been met? If that is the case it is not likely to be an interpretative evaluation project. However, if the purpose of the evaluation is or can be reframed in such a manner as to ask how the person involved in the project can understand and accomplish the end-states, then the project is potentially an interpretative evaluation.

After the evaluation question has been articulated, a series of additional questions need to be asked and answered. What data to collect? How might the data be collected? And what is the most appropriate and helpful way to present the findings?

To gain some sense of how an evaluation may unfold, allow me to use this imagined scenario. Let's say that you are asked to evaluate the effectiveness of a community-based project to reduce unwise decisions among youths regarding drugs and alcohol. There are some straightforward measures that can be taken. For example, you might count the number of arrests for underage drinking the year before the project began and at the end of the first year of the project. While it is likely that this measure is one that might be taken, it is also likely the evaluation may find a very small change (if any) at the end of one year. Other measures that may be taken will of course depend on the nature of the project. But that is the point. If the project is built on increasing community assets (Kretzmann *et al.* 2005), then the data you need to collect will be based on knowing the extent that the individuals and the community have increased their assets. In turn, that means that you have to have planned ahead to be sure you have a way to access that information. The point is that evaluation questions, while not given specifically, are embedded in the nature and values of the project. One additional and perhaps obvious issue – evaluation starts at the beginning of the project, not at the end.

Why would you want to do an interpretative evaluation project? Isn't the purpose of an evaluation project to satisfy the project coordinator or the funding agency that the project has met it goals or accomplished its purposes? If that's the case isn't it more appropriate to conduct a traditional evaluation, a neo-positivist evaluation? Perhaps that may be the case in some evaluations; however, if there is a concern that includes how the project works, how it affects the persons receiving services and the people delivering the services, if you are looking to understand the agency or the participants as they engage with each other, then it seems appropriate to conduct an interpretative evaluation.

Here is an example of what I mean. Asked to evaluate an ongoing program involving university-student tutors' effectiveness in helping students in a course on anatomy and physiology, there were two questions. First, did participation in tutoring help students in mastering the material and gaining a better grade? The second question concerned how the tutoring process worked (Morehouse *et al.* 2009). The orientation of this question was to better understand the process so as to eventually be able to improve the effectiveness of the university-student tutors. In order to accomplish the second goal understanding the week-to-week tutoring sessions as they unfolded was necessary – knowing the final results would help only minimally.

Transforming researchable ideas into interpretative questions

With this list of researchable ideas at the ready, the next task is to frame these ideas in an interpretative context. This means that the question should be sensitive to action, meaning-making, and agency within a specific milieu. Here are several examples from published studies. The first example is a qualitative study of pre-med students. The stated goal of the study is "to explore, delve into, and develop a better understanding of the goal orientation of a group of college level science students who were preparing for careers in medicine" (Horowitz 2010: 218). In a quantitative study of the effects of conflict on defensive interpersonal behavior using scripted-real time dialogues, Westerman and Steen asked whether participants' responses would be less coordinated in the conflict condition than in the nonconflict condition (Westerman and Steen 2009: 394). Lovett and Pillow (2010) explore children's and adults' explanations of interpersonal actions. Their study makes four hypotheses. I summarize them as follows. Children and adults would provide situational and mental state explanations, references to an actor's goals to explain action would increase with age, older children and adults will attribute less apparent goals to others and explanations would vary based on the social context of the action.

Assets inventory

Three assets relating to coming up with ideas for an inquiry project are interest, knowledge, and resources. In order to conceptualize, initiate, and implement an interpretative inquiry project, the inquirer needs to bring to bear this set of assets. These assets will also sustain the ongoing research efforts.

Interest, and its twin sister curiosity, are commodities available to us as a part of our humanity. While interest is not something that needs to be acquired, it does need to be directed and nurtured. As one begins to think about an inquiry project, I recommend a search of what captures your attention and an examination of the things you are passionate about. Interest may be the most important asset for beginning the project. While it may seem at first glance that resources or knowledge might be the determining asset in choosing a project, my experience is that a project that captures one's interest will allow one to gain the necessary knowledge and muster the other resources needed to complete a project.

That said, occasionally the availability of resources may spark a sustaining interest in a project, but that is more the exception than the rule, at least in my experience. An inquiry project demands a good deal of time and energy, and it is difficult maintaining the effort without an abiding interest. Interest is a self-renewing commodity the deeper one gets into the topic and the greater the need to contextualize one's findings, and the broader one looks the greater the desire for more in-depth knowledge. Philip Phenix (1970) provides an insight into the self-sustaining nature of an inquiry project. Although Phenix is writing about the nature of academic disciplines his analysis applies at least metaphorically to inquiry. He states that a discipline works by first simplifying the topic under investigation. With a simplified, but not simplistic, understanding of the topic, we then move to what he calls synthetic coordination. A discipline is a synthetic structure of concepts made possible by the discrimination of similarities through analysis. We then place what is known into a hierarchy of ideas as a unity-in-difference (Phenix 1970: 347). We use these simplified concepts to weave together ideas into a coherent whole. This process of analysis and connecting into coherent wholes, leads to what he labeled "the lure of discovery." By moving back and forth from analysis to synthesis we are drawn deeper into the topic and pulled to connect the specific findings to their wider contexts (Morehouse 2000:86). Our curiosity is thus fueled.

Knowledge as an asset related to an inquiry project will be explored next. Having a broad base of knowledge about the research topic provides a context for library searches, the selection of key words, a list of potential authors who have contributed to the field, and a framework into which one can place and evaluate research articles. Novices in a field of inquiry are faced with a dilemma; they do not know what to look for and may not recognize it when they find it. There is a reason that university courses in research are usually offered to upper-class undergraduates or graduate students.

However, new inquirers should be reminded that they do know enough to start and that all of us have limited knowledge. Jerome Bruner's comments about distributive knowledge, that is, knowledge beyond what is confined in a single mind is helpful here.

> A person's knowledge … is not just in one's own head, in "person solo," but in the notes that one has put into accessible notebooks, in books with underlined passages on one's shelves, in the handbooks one has learned how to consult, in the information sources one has hitched up to the computer, in the friends one can call up to get a reference or a "steer" and so on endlessly.
>
> (Bruner 1990: 106)

As a new inquirer you can rely on your colleagues and on senior researchers to provide helpful hints, direction, and support. Also, it should be noted that not all the advantages lie on the side of the most knowledgeable person. In some ways, inquirers new to research and evaluation have an advantage. The advantage comes about because there is a tricky relationship between previous knowledge and new learning: old knowledge can sometimes inhibit or distort new learning, thus the person new to the field of inquiry may see connections and threads that the "old hand" may not notice. Those new to an area of research as well as veteran scholars need to stay open to changing one's mind and allow new information to shape or reshape what one already knows.

Research exercise 6.5: Resource inventory

Assessing one's resources has two purposes. The first purpose is to find the extent of the resources you already have. The second purpose it to figure out how to expand and extend those resources. Physical resources may include, but are not limited to, things such as computers, audio and visual recording devices, and still cameras. Conceptual resources may include assessment instruments, training manuals, library search engines, and databases.

Personal resources may include research mentors and colleagues, professional contacts, and social networks. This list of resources will of necessity be a general list, as you have not yet developed your research question. This exercise is intended to illustrate what you are aware of in terms of general resources and will provide a rubric as you revisit Table 6.2 after you have stated your research question(s).

Resources come in many forms. A place to begin is with taking stock of your resources. My experience is that often one has more resources that one may initially think. Resources are physical, conceptual, and personal. Some of them were mentioned in the Bruner quote above. For an inquiry project, resources also include the availability of places and people to involve in the project. This includes inquiry participants as well as fellow inquirers. An inquirer needs to know whom to contact, whom to encourage, and who can provide leads to other resources. One resource leads to another resource. As researchers we need to take advantage of the resources we have, and build from there.

Table 6.2 Cataloging resources

	What are they?	How can I access them?	How important are they to this project?
Physical resources			
Conceptual resources			
Personal resources			
Resources related to accessing a population for the project			
Resources related to gaining information about participants			
Resources related to addressing the research question (data collection)			
Resources related to data analysis			

Even with the resources that you have listed above, resource development takes patience. To find the necessary resources to complete a project, begin with those resources that are at hand. Each of us has greater availability to resources than would appear at first glance. For me that key is the courage to ask others for help and to take a chance on using what is in front of me. For example, the first effort at finding a potential research site may not be successful. Success is gained by trying again and sometimes by rethinking in some small or large way one or more elements of your project. The very people who turned down your request to conduct the project at their site may be willing to suggest a similar site for your project. It may also be instructive to ask the reasons for refusing your project. The answer may lead to a way that you can alter one or two elements of your project so that the project becomes acceptable to the gatekeepers of the site. It may also be a matter of your not explaining the project clearly enough to those gatekeepers.

Summary

Sometimes ideas for research and research questions come easily. Sometimes one knows what one is going to research long before one even embarks on the planning process. An evaluation project may be foisted on you by the requirements of a grant or a responsibility given to you by your boss. Under those circumstances, the task may be somewhat different from the task outlined here. Your job will be to determine whether or not this project fits under the rubric of an interpretative inquiry or whether some other orientation is a better fit. My sense is that even under these quite different circumstances much of this chapter will be helpful in sorting out your project. Specifically, the discussion of evaluation projects addresses these issues. Now I move on to sampling, data collection, data analysis, and writing up the project.

Chapter 7

Launching the inquiry

Literature search and review, problem statement, design, and sample

This chapter covers three main parts of an inquiry project: the literature search and review, the problem statement, and the inquiry sample. These three topics are not usually included in the same chapter. I have chosen to place them together for two somewhat related reasons. First, a search and review of the literature leads naturally to the writing of the problem statement as well as to shaping the sample in several important ways. As your research question is an interpretative one, your search of the literature is likely to lead to large quasi-experimental studies, surveys, and small qualitative studies. The shaping of your topic may occur simultaneously with consideration of who should participate in your study, that is, your sample.

The other reason for combining literature review, problem statement, and sample relates to the organization of the rest of the book. My belief is that data collection and data analysis are conceptually connected and therefore better addressed in a single chapter. An integrated data collection and data analysis chapter better represents how the two processes work together in actual inquiry projects.

The design of an interpretative project begins by the writing of an inquiry question, moves to data collection considerations, and then looks at approaches to data analysis.

Literature search

A literature search is a systematic search for information on a specific issue or problem but also includes the collection and organization of that information. I will explore each of these tasks separately under this heading of literature search. It goes without saying that literature searches have changed over the past 25 years, as have methods for collecting and organizing information; however, some of the old ways of searching, collecting, and organizing data are still useful. Therefore, I will present a mixture of new and old approaches to both areas.

While I will present a step-by-step linear approach to the literature search as an instructional tool, the process is often messier and less straightforward. With that caveat in mind, the literature search begins with your research question. With the research question in front of you, look to the key words in your question. Your university library is likely to have an article search engine available to all university personnel. These come in a variety of forms and under different names.

My library uses a search engine called Academic Search Complete by EBSCOhost. There is a line of four blank spaces followed by a box entitled "select a field (optional)." Within that box there are the following options, among others: Author, Title, and Subject Terms. On the left side with the four blank boxes there is a choice of "and," "or," and "not." These prompts are very helpful as they allow you widen your search by selecting "or" and narrow your search by using "and." Using the "not" option can eliminate unnecessary titles. Using "not" is metaphorically like clearing the noise from the environment.

When you find your first article that is a good match for your topic, look under the abstract in any journal and you will find the phrase "Key Words." The key words section of the article can be a great source for continuing your search. It follows that the key words from one study are likely to lead to other studies that are similar to the one that you found helpful. By using these words and using the prompts of "and," "or," and "not" you can move efficiently through large amounts of research. The other valuable tool for continuing your search is an old fashioned one: the bibliography. When I read a research article that I think I will use I like to note the citations that interest me. I stop and turn to the references or bibliography and put a check mark next to the appropriate reference. I may or may not look-up this reference, but when I look at the article for a second or third reading, if the article still seems important I will do a library (on-line) search or, if it is a book, I will find it in the library.

For efficient reading of research articles, begin with a careful reading of the abstract. You should be able to determine if the article is worth reading in its entirety by reading the abstract. Once you have decided that the article falls within the parameters of your search, there is a strategy for reading a research article that I have found helpful. By exploring that strategy, I will outline the structure of a typical research article. Following the abstract a research article begins with a review of the literature. In most cases this section of the article is not labeled. This section may be organized in several different ways; usually beginning by providing information regarding the importance of this research (this will look something like your problem statement when you eventually write it). Why the issue is important to the general public, that is, its social context is usually addressed first. Why it is important to the professional members of the field of inquiry will also be found in these opening paragraphs. Once the problem is situated socially and professionally, the review may take several different approaches to presenting an overview of what has been already accomplished in the research. Some reviews will take a thematic approach, exploring the major themes and subthemes of the research projects. Another approach is to organize the review by research methods used to study the phenomenon. The organizational strategy of either approach will likely include thematic and methods assessments but will have a slightly different feel to them.

This later approach often includes a critique of these methods. With either approach the goal is both to provide an overview of what is known and what is still to be learned about the topic. By exploring what is known and what needs to be discovered, the author leads the reader to his or her research question(s). A method section follows. This section tells the reader how the researcher is going to address the question(s) she or he has raised. Next come the results, followed by a discussion. The discussion contextualizes the research and points to what still needs to be known on this topic. The references or bibliography usually end the article but in some cases there will be an appendix with additional information.

In selecting the articles to read, first focus on what is most important to you. The abstract should allow you to select what to read most carefully following our initial search. While you will need to carefully read all the articles you eventually select for your review of the literature, this initial reading is a part of a search process. At this stage you may be more interested in the methods section than in the results section. Alternately the review of the literature and the discussion may have the information you need to decide if this article should be set aside for re-reading. I am suggesting a three-step tactic for reading as a part of your search strategy. First read the abstract carefully. The abstract is your first cut. Based on reading the abstract you are likely to know if the article fits your overall search strategy. Next read one or two sections of the paper somewhat carefully to make a tentative decision about the usefulness of the article. This reading should confirm that the selected article is one that will be useful as you write your research proposal. While you are culling the article be sure to note the ones that you are not using. A simple list of authors and titles with a statement like "not useful," or "possibly useful" will help you to retrieve an article later. Sometimes you may even have a category such as "possible for a future project."

Thus far I have focused on research articles. There are two additional types of articles that you are likely to come across in your search: theory articles and reviews of the literature. Leading scholars in the field often use theoretical articles to frame their research and the research of others in a theoretical perspective. An example of this is an article by McAdams and Pals (2006) called "A new big five: Fundamental principles for an integrative science of personality" which presents a new perspective on how to organize theories of personality. An article such as this provides a person seeking to understand the literature on personality with an overarching perspective enabling them to place their own work into a large context. "Self-determination theory and the facilitation of intrinsic motivation, social development, and well-being" (Ryan and Deci 2000) provides a context for the authors' work as well as related theories on self-determination. Sometimes the best way for a new inquirer to gain a perspective on the field is to consult handbooks in their area of interest such as *Handbook of Competence and Motivation* (Elliott and Dweck 2005), *Handbook of Child Development*, fifth edition (four volumes) (Damon 1998), *Handbook of Child Psychology*, sixth edition (Damon and Lerner 2006), *Routledge International Handbook of Creative Learning* (Sefton-Green, Thomson, Bresler, and Jones, Eds 2011), *The Routledge International Handbook of the Sociology of Education* (Apple, Ball, and Gandin (eds.) 2009), *The Routledge International Handbook of Critical Education* (Apple, Au, and Gandin (eds.) 2009), and *The Routledge international companion to multicultural education* (Banks Ed 2009). Trade books can also be used to gain a sense of the big picture for your research topic but are not likely to provide the detailed explanation of specific research projects needed to complete a solid literature search. Textbooks may also provide context, but are generally not good as sources for research articles. In addition to their value as context providers, both textbooks and trade books usually have bibliographies that may lead to solid research articles for your review.

Literature review

A review of the literature should include an overview of the relevant scholarship that bears directly on the inquiry topic. "A review should make clear how the study contributes to, challenges, and/or extends theory practice, methodology, research results, knowledge and/or understanding within an arena of inquiry" (AERA 2006).

As you begin to assemble your review of the literature, select from a group of articles that you have read with some care some articles for re-reading with an eye to including them in your review of the literature. After reading and taking marginal notes, I have found it helpful to use a strategy adopted from David Perkins' (1986) book, *Knowledge as Design*. In it he writes that knowledge can be thought of as a design, just as a building has a design. He argues that any design can be understood by asking the four design questions: What is the purpose? What is the structure? What is a model case? What is the argument? I am going to use these questions as a framework for conducting a literature review.

The purpose of a literature review in the writing of a research proposal is to gain a command of the research, theoretical, and methodological literature on your topic. Notice that the purpose is stated in terms of what the inquirer is to gain. When writing up the results of your study the purpose shifts to demonstrating a command of the inquiry topic to the reader. Gaining a command of the topic may include the following areas:

1   defining the problem by examining what has been accomplished so far;
2   gaining a sense of the way the research has been conducted (methods of data collection and data analysis);
3   finding gaps in the research, that is, are there unanswered as well as unasked questions; and
4   determining what else needs to be done.

The structure of a typical research review of the literature will be used to both illustrate how the research review appears in its final form as well as a tool for writing a review of the literature. The structure of a review of the literature may be seen in its several parts: initial question(s), framing the content to be reviewed conceptually, analyzing the articles both individually and as a whole and relating the review to your specific research question.

A model case provides a benchmark for what a review might look like. I will present an outline of a model review with some features allowing for both a big picture and transparency. The goal of the outline is to offer enough of the elements of the review to see both its structure and some of the details that round out the review.

In the argument section, I will present a perspective on how a review of the literature for a completed article is similar to and different from a review of literature for an inquiry proposal. Perkins (1986), in his definition of an argument as it relates to knowledge as design, suggests that an argument can been seen as the structure in service of the purpose. In other words, an argument illustrates how the way something is put together (structure) makes clear the intention (purpose) of that design. By comparing a review of the literature for a completed project and a project proposal, the structure and the purpose of a review should become clear.

Initial question to review framework

In conducting your literature search, you had a question in mind. That search question now becomes a framework for your review. Your initial question is a place to start, but it may be modified as you enter deeper into your review. Keep your goal in front of you as you work. Your research question is a guide, that is, it is neither carved in stone nor totally malleable. Your research question is a review framework allowing one to demonstrate a command of what research has been conducted on this topic by contextualizing it, comparing similar and contradictory research, and different research methods. The ultimate goal is to construct an argument that leads to your research – both your research proposal and your completed research project.

Organizing your review findings

Remember that your review in some ways makes a contribution to knowledge. It will provide the reader and perhaps more importantly you, as the inquirer, with a rich understanding of your topic. The contribution of the literature may add to the understanding of a theory, a new perspective on method, or a deeper or nuanced understanding of the research topics. Examine your accumulated studies and organize them into an argument. An argument organizes information by beginning with a premise, presenting support for that premise, following with a counterargument, and ending with a rebuttal.

A review of the literature should follow a clear logic, tracing a path through the previously conducted research, and connecting each piece of research to the previous one. Your premise should connect to some theoretical perspective or perspectives. This logic may vary somewhat depending on the kind of review you are conducting. If, for example, the study is closely related to practice, the inquirer needs to make clear what the practical concerns are and how the existing research informs practice. If the study looks at research where there is a current lack of information, the reviewer needs to make clear the topic's importance and how the study intends to fill the gap (AERA 2006).

This may seem oversimplified, to organize a review of the literature as an argument, but I would argue that all well-written reviews have this format as the skeleton for a review of the literature. As with most simplified teaching tools, as one uses the tool one gets better at using it, making modifications and improvements along the way. However, even the most sophisticated reviews will, I think, maintain this skeleton.

Problem statement

The problem formulation should provide a clear statement of the purpose. A well-written problem statement provides the structure and the scope of the study. It describes the issue(s) the study addresses. The problem statement also situates the research topic in context while describing the approach taken to addressing it. It also provides an explanation of why the project is important to be addressed (AERA 2006). With the problem statement completed, it is now time to organize the sample, but first one word about the placement of the problem statement. I have intentionally placed the problem statement after the review of the literature, but when you write the research proposal it will come before the review. However, I think that it makes sense to write the problem statement after you have written your review. At the very least, you should have your review reading completed and a working outline for the review before you write your final problem statement.

Design

Design is a specific phase in the preparation of an inquiry project. Just as questions from Perkins' Knowledge as Design (1986) provided a guide to understanding and organizing the research literature, the design questions are also helpful in the design phase of a research or evaluation project. A way to determine which inquiry design fits the needs of a particular project is to ask and answer Perkins' questions. Following the same steps presented earlier in this chapter will aid in determining the design of the project.

Stating the purpose of the inquiry helps to determine which of the major research designs one selects: quantitative, qualitative, or mixed method design. Figuring out the structure of the inquiry further defines how the project will be conducted. Specifically, the structure is about how the inquiry is put together; it is about the details of how, when, and where the data will be collected. The review of the literature will aid the researcher in finding a model case. A model case in this instance is a project that has met all or most of the requirements that the new project is intending to address. The argument re-examines the structure and the model case to explore the extent to which these components support the purpose of the study.

Three design issues – single case study, longitudinal case study, or cross-sectional case study

In an interpretative inquiry questions of design are colored by the focus on agency, action, and meaning-making. What that means as we plan a project is keeping in mind a contextual evolving understanding rather than an isolated, overly limited, static proof. With that orientation in mind, here is a way to approach the design of an inquiry.

The design of an inquiry project includes the plans and the procedures for the project, beginning with the underlying assumptions of the project that shape the detail methods of data collection and analysis to be used (Creswell 2009). There are three major inquiry designs: qualitative, quantitative, and mixed. Briefly, qualitative designs focus more on understanding people's words and actions without using statistical measures. The focus is to find themes within the context of interviews, observations, and documents. Quantitative designs use numbers and statistics to gain an understanding of persons and events. Mixed method designs use qualitative and quantitative data to understand the phenomena under investigation. I have initially defined methods somewhat generally in order to now place them within an interpretative context.

As the design phase unfolds, three sets of questions arise: questions of the inquiry problem, questions regarding personal experience and knowledge, and questions of audience. The review of the research and the way that the research problem has been stated addresses the first question. In other words, reviewing what has been researched on the chosen topic has already partially formed your design. The reading of the articles and books for the review of literature will help to delineate some of the design questions. As one reads the research one needs to look closely at the design of the projects as well as how well the research questions were asked. Careful reading of the past research is likely to show gaps, partially answered questions, and important issues that may have been left unexamined. These questions will have been addressed using Perkins' knowledge as design questions (1986).

The inquirer's personal experience also shapes the research design. The experiences that shape one's choices of design are not limited to research or evaluation experience. Your experience and knowledge of the topic of inquiry will also influence the design. On a very basic level, a person with little experience and somewhat limited knowledge of the field of inquiry is likely to begin with a simple design, while a person with more experience and knowledge will likely lean toward a more complicated or sophisticated design. This is especially true if the project under consideration is a second or third project conducted by the researcher or the research team. This increasing complexity is due in part to the increased confidence one has in one's ability as a researcher, but it is also because the immersion in the literature for the completion of the first project coupled with a clearer understanding of the issues to be studied increases with experience.

A personal experience will illustrate this point. A research team that I headed began with an interest in how the research of Carol Dweck on theories of intelligence and Noel Entwistle's work on deep and surface learning related to the outcome of students who sought tutoring in an anatomy and physiology class as a part of a nursing curriculum. We specifically were interested in how the tutors' profile with regard to theories of intelligence and their orientation toward study would influence the profiles of the tutees in these two areas and the scores that the students received on their final exams. This was a quantitative study with pre-post measures and simple inferential statistical analysis (Morehouse *et al.* 2007). This led the team (now expanded with two additional researchers) to a more elaborate study looking at the process of tutoring via video recordings of the tutoring session in addition to looking at the student and tutor profiles on theories of intelligence and orientation toward study. This second study uses pre-post measure plus an analysis of the video recorded session for orientation to study, theories of intelligence and types of questions asked by both tutors and tutees (Morehouse *et al.* 2010).

Sample

Almost no inquiries include all the participants in the study, with the exception of some small qualitative research or evaluation projects using intact groups. Participants for an inquiry are selected. The preferred manner of sampling for a qualitative study is called purposive sampling, meaning the sample is selected on purpose in a systematic way. Usually, quantitative samples, especially for experimental studies, are selected randomly. With a random sample, participants are not only chosen at random but have an equal chance of being in the experimental or control group. In quasi-experimental studies intact groups most often make up the participants.

Planning your inquiry begins with the construction of a sample. In traditional quantitative research, the purpose of the sample is to ensure that your findings are representative of the larger population, ideally constructed by selecting participants at random. Qualitative researchers, on the other hand, often pick participants who are likely to aid in understanding a particular phenomenon. The participants are, therefore, picked on purpose. Interpretative inquiry seeks to understand the actions of persons in particular situations. The sample you construct should help you to understand some important actions and how individuals are involved in those actions. The challenge of a project comes not only in selecting appropriate participants but also in ensuring that the quantitative and qualitative data are oriented to understanding the actions of the participants in the same or very similar situations.

The qualitative researcher seeks maximum variation rather than a random sample. This is called a purposive sample. A purposive sample, as any other sample, seeks to gain a picture of a larger group by examining a smaller group. One needs a large population in order to get a random sample that will be sound. As qualitative studies generally have a small sample, how can one be assured that this small sample represents a larger group of potential participants? The answer is to seek maximum variation. This may be done in several ways. One technique is called "snowballing." This technique begins by selecting several participants thought to represent the extremes of the population and perhaps a participant in the middle of those extremes. For example if one is going to examine study habits of first year university students, one might begin by selecting enrolled students in the upper quarter of their secondary school class, and one student enrolled student at the low end of their secondary school classes. After interviewing those students, ask them to recommend someone for the study who is like them in terms of student habits and someone who is not at all like them in terms of study habits. Continue this process, interviewing each pair of students until you are no longer getting new information.

Research exercise 7.1: Constructing a purposive sample for a qualitative inquiry

You intend to explore student reaction to a new dormitory on campus. You want to get a range of opinions from students who are now living in the new dorm as well as from students who live on campus but who are not living in the new building. You also wish to have a sample that matches the percentages of males and females on campus. There are about 200 students living in the new dorm.

How would you go about creating a purposive sample?

Here is one way to collect this sample. Some of the possible categories for the sample are listed; the number to be included in each category is to be determined.

- Students living in the new dorm _____
- Students living on campus but not in the new dorm _____
- Males _____
- Females _____
- First year students _____
- Upper class students _____

Are there other groups or individuals that should be selected to ensure that your sample represents the range of students in each category? In determining the number of students to be included in each category some of the things to be considered are the demographics of the university. Should your number match the numbers of students in the university or should you strive for equal or nearly equal numbers in each category?

Using this as a template, and your own potential project, develop a purposive sample. Important issues to be concerned with are how are the purposes of your inquiry addressed by the inclusion or exclusion of persons for your sample? Are there considerations for selecting specific people? In the example above, should you make sure to include students who transferred from another university or students who lived in other dorms on campus? To state this concern more generally, with what you know about your inquiry questions, whose opinion would you like to be sure to include in your sample?

Johnson *et al.* (1995) explored campus life by looking at students in sororities and fraternities, college dorms as well as students living at home for an alternative sampling approach. As this was a qualitative study, the researchers selected 19 freshmen students. The largest number of students (nine) lived in Greek sorority or fraternity houses. A slightly smaller number of students (six) lived in campus dormitories. Four lived at home with parents and commuted to campus. All of the students in the study were enrolled in their first academic term at the university. The data was collected by recording weekly discussions where they gave their views about their first term experiences (p. 340). See Maykut and Morehouse (1994: 56–63) for a detailed look at sampling for a qualitative study.

If the data is going to be primarily quantitative then a larger sample is suggested (see Talarico 2009) for an interesting look at the unique memories and first time events as experienced by first year university students. If all the participants in the research or evaluation project can be included, they should be. If including all participants is not possible, a random sample is recommended. If the data is qualitative and quantitative, a smaller purposive sample might be combined with a more inclusive one, perhaps including the entire pool of participants or a percentage of participants selected at random.

Research exercise 7.2: Constructing a sample for a mixed methods study

Selecting a sample for a mixed method inquiry depends, to some degree, on the overall relationship between the qualitative and quantitative data you plan to collect. Using the project outlined earlier (research exercise 7.1), assume that you are most interested in finding out the depth and range of student opinion and you wish to focus on how the new dorm has influenced their study for year-end examinations. You are also concerned about their opinions about the new dorm in general, including a rating of general satisfaction, change over time (a retrospective on their first impression, mid-term impression, and end of term impression) and their assessment of dorm staff over time (using the same time periods and method). You plan to collect the general opinions about dorm satisfaction in a paper and pencil survey.

How should one go about constructing or selecting a sample for an interpretative inquiry? As an interpretative inquiry looks to understanding action and agency within ongoing situations, the sample should reflect those considerations. Intact groups and individuals involved in an ongoing activity fit the bill. If the study uses primarily qualitative data (audio/video recordings, interviews, document analysis) the sample will need to be somewhat limited, and therefore the method for selection is likely to be intentional, a purposive sample.

Are there other groups or individuals that should be selected to ensure that your sample represents the range of students in each category?

Using this as a template and your own potential project, develop a purposive sample. Important issues to be concerned with are how are purposes of your inquiry addressed by the inclusion or exclusion of persons for your sample? Are there considerations for selecting specific people? In the example above, should you make sure to include students who transferred from another university or students who lived in other dorms on campus? To state this concern more generally, with what you know about your inquiry questions, whose opinion would you like to be sure to include in your sample?

In a series of published articles, Christopher Day and colleagues presented the results of a three-year longitudinal mix methods study of teachers' lives, work, and effectiveness. While those beginning interpretative inquiry are not likely to undertake a study as complex as the one undertaken by Christopher Day and colleagues (Day *et al.* 2008; Sammons *et al.* 2007) there is still much to learn regarding sampling from this study. In this study, the authors examined teachers and school effectiveness and teachers' lives over time. It described and explored variations in teachers' work, lives, and their effects on pupils' educational outcomes. The study brought together research in two areas: mainly quantitative research on teacher (school) effectiveness and mainly qualitative research on teachers' work and lives on the other hand (Sammons *et al.* 2007). The sampling strategy used to collect the data is what is of importance here.

The sampling process began with a survey of 100 schools and 300 teachers. Schools were selected for the study based on diverse socioeconomic levels and a range of attainment scores and included schools in rural, suburban, and urban locations. Test scores over three years were collected for all the pupils from the selected schools in grades two, six and nine. Age, experience, gender, subject specialty (English and mathematics at secondary level), and length of service were used to select teachers. As the strategy for selecting schools and teachers in the Day and colleagues' study (Day *et al.* 2008; Sammons *et al.* 2007) is similar to the approach outlined in research exercises 7.1 and 7.2, you are encouraged to read one or both of the reports in order to gain a fuller picture of both the process and product of sample building for a larger study.

Summary

By including a literature search and review with the writing of a problem statement and the building of an inquiry sample, I hoped to illustrate that proposal writing is an integrated whole that unfolds in a more or less linear manner, but with occasional moves back and some opportunities to leap ahead. I would call the process of proposal writing described here as an organic pathway with stepping-stones through a garden path rather than a set of steps that lead steadily upward. I hope the path I have provided not only leads you through the proposal writing process but give you some flexibility to make your own path.

Chapter 8

Data collection and data analysis

How does one capture the ongoing action by agents who are seeking meaning? A reminder of the definition of agency will help answer that question. Argyris *et al.* (2010) cite an article published in1995 by Hayes-Roth where he defines agents as persons who "continually perform three functions: perception of dynamic conditions in the environment; action to affect conditions in the environment; and reasoning to interpret perceptions, solve problems, draw inferences, and determine action" (p. 298). An interpretative inquiry attempts to capture the actions that an agent is involved in as she works with, responds to, or changes the environment as well as the thinking used by the agent to reason, solve problems, draw inferences, and determine action. The meaning of words, Wittgenstein has taught us, cannot be defined by pointing to them but can only be realized in the context of human activities (Harré and Tissaw 2005: 73).

What quantitative, qualitative, and mixed methods studies in the interpretative vein share is an orientation to human understanding based on intentionality (doing something directed beyond one's self and normatively constrained) and resulting from a lifetime of interpersonal interaction (Harré and van Langenhove 1999). Given that perspective, it is reasonable that a research plan and the selection of a research method are considerably intertwined. To sort out the questions related to design I begin by dividing the strategies for inquiry into three areas: quantitative strategies, qualitative strategies, and mixed methods strategies. As a part of a quantitative strategy, one can choose to conduct a survey project or an experimental project. Surveys provide mathematical descriptions of trends, attitudes, and opinions of a group of participants. One can conduct a single incident survey, use a cross-sectional approach, or a longitudinal approach. Alternately one can conduct a single case study using quantitative measures and an ABAB design or a quasi-experimental design. A true experimental design is an unlikely interpretative project.

Many researchers and evaluators argue that quantitative research fits into a positivist orientation. However, Michael Westerman (2005) makes clear that quantitative inquiry can be, and maybe even almost always is, within the interpretative inquiry family. He begins by stating why interpretative inquiry is a good thing. He argues against a fundamental split between the observer and the world. The person is always already involved in meaningful practical activities in the world, not a spectator fundamentally separate from the world. Adopting a hermeneutic perspective based on practical activity has fundamental implications for psychology. It leads to recognizing that people are always *in medias res* (i.e. in the middle of things), as Fischer and Bidell (1998) aptly put it. Therefore, instead of trying to understand psychological phenomena by putting together accounts from "external" events, behavioral responses, and "inner" processes such as perceptions, cognitions, and feelings (which mediate responses to events) – with all of these terms treated as if they were isolatable, building block constituents of our accounts that are more basic than the practical activities they compose – we should start with what a person is doing, for example, building a house, enjoying the company of friends, or trying to create museum exhibits that are of interest to viewers.

I go back again to a study by Michael Westerman and Edward Steen (2009) to illustrate how one can work within a quantitative data collection methodology and maintain an interpretative orientation to the overall project. Relational theories of defense and discourse analysis are used to capture responses from individuals by utilizing open-ended scenarios to generate quantitative data. The data was collected with a focus on the interaction of the participants, not from a snapshot, one-off data bite. The key data was to count discourse breaches. A discourse breach was defined as occurring when a person changed the direction of the conversation in order to circumvent the possible consequences of maintaining the discourse. The researchers were able to capture how individuals respond within a relational dyad to conflict and non-conflict. The discourse breaches were counted and compared under conflict and non-conflict situations.

Most qualitative data collection methods are designed to work within that orientation. Audio and video recording of classroom activities, therapy sessions, work meetings, and planning sessions are specific examples of interpretative data that privilege agency, action, and meaning-making that is intentional and grounded in extended interpersonal interaction. Interviews that are conducted in an open-ended manner focus on the agents engaged in meaning-making regarding other people's actions and ideas, as well as their own attempt to capture meaning-making. A good example from a book-length project which catches the act of meaning-making is *Women's Ways of Knowing* (Belenky *et al.* 1986). The authors meet the challenge of how to collect qualitative data within the interpretative framework by using a semi-structured interview schedule that is framed to aid in understanding three key elements of intellectual development: self, voice, and mind.

Rom Harré's work on positioning theory is another example of how to employ qualitative methods in an interpretative framework (Harré and van Langenhove 1999). Positioning theory is the study of patterns of mutual and contestable rights and obligations expressed in the speech and acts of individuals and groups. With its emphasis on intentionality and a focus on understanding persons within the context of lifeline interaction, position theory falls within the parameters of interpretative inquiry.

What can be drawn from these examples as principles to aid in constructing an approach to data collection in an interpretative inquiry? First, meaning is concrete regardless of whether it is gleaned from quantitative or qualitative data. Second, inquiry is interpretative. Finally, understanding action, agency, and meaning-making are the primary goals of inquiry in education and the human sciences.

Tools for interpretative data collection

Examining the use of data collection tools begins with a definition of each of the tools and moves on to provide some details about how and when to use each of the specific data collection tools. I begin with those tools used primarily in qualitative inquiry followed by tools used in quantitative and mixed methods projects.

Qualitative measures

In-depth interviews

This method of data collection is perhaps the most widely used of all qualitative measures. An in-depth interview is an open-ended and semi-structured exploration of a topic engaging one person at a time with an interviewer. The openness of the interview begins with the framing of the focus of inquiry and the first question in the schedule. The interviewee is considered a co-researcher on the topic of inquiry, so it is essential to let the interviewee in on what the interviewer wants to understand. On the other hand, as the goal is to find out the perspective of the interviewee, it is essential that the first question allows the interviewee to set the agenda for the interview. It is not untypical for the interview to begin by asking, "What stands out for you over x time period regarding the issue framed in the focus of inquiry?" This first question allows the interviewee to explore an answer to the focus of inquiry more-or-less on his or her own terms. After the first question a series of probes follows. The probe questions are usually written out in advance but held in abeyance until after the interviewee has completed her first answer. The interviewer then asks a follow-up question depending on the answer to the first question. Questions in an in-depth interview schedule are usually organized in sections. The tradition in these interviews is to end by asking the interviewee if there are any questions that should have been asked. This is more than a courtesy. As qualitative inquiry is emergent, asking the participant what else might have been explored in the study may expand the scope of the inquiry in valuable ways. For a model interview see Figure 8.1.

Group interviews/focus group questionnaires

A group interview and a focus group are more-or-less synonymous. Focus group is the term often used in a business setting or for gaining the perspective on various topics for political candidates. Therefore I prefer to use the term group interview as a more neutral research term. Group interviews have from 10 to 20 participants and one or two interviewers. It can be helpful to have two interviewers especially for larger groups. A group interview schedule, like the in-depth interview schedule, is open-ended and participant shaped. It is therefore valuable to begin with a question stem that begins with "What stands out for you regarding …?" In a group interview there are fewer questions as the individuals feed off each other's comments in a conversational manner. It is helpful for the interviewer(s) to occasionally summarize the sense of the group consensus, if one emerges. Below is an example of a group interview that I conducted. The context for the interview was a part of an evaluation of a four-day mini-college experience designed to acquaint high school students with some elements of college teaching and more generally of college life. The overall purpose was to encourage students who might not have considered attending college to understand that college is accessible to them and that they have the potential to be admitted to and eventually complete some post-secondary education.

Group Interview
Precollege Scholarship Program

Introduction

Introduction of self and what will happen.

Let the group know that although we are calling it an interview, it is really more of a conversation. We are having a conversation to find out about how the Precollege Scholarship Program went from their perspective.

Consent

I am asking you to participate in an interview that will last about 25 to 30 minutes. All of the interviews that are conducted for this project will be video-recorded and then transcribed for reading by the project team. It is important for us to capture your words and ideas and using the video recorder will allow us to do this. May I have your permission to tape record this group interview? [Turn on the video-recorder.]

Only members of our research team will have access to the interview transcripts. We will be using the transcribed interviews to carefully study what you have to say about the Precollege Scholarship Program.

Please know that you can withdraw as a participant at any time.

Focus of Inquiry

We hope to learn more about your experiences as well as what you have learned during this program. Additionally, we are interested in finding out about your attitudes and concerns about the nature of college and about your future.

Questions
- As you look back at the five days that you were here at Viterbo, what stands out for you?
    - Now probe for different items.
        - If they did not mention anything academic ask: Did any of your classes stand out? Good or bad?
            - Any activities within the class that you remember as being interesting? How about boring?
        - If they did not mention anything about recreation, ask about evening activities and free time.
        - Sometimes we have ideas about how something is before we even experience it. What college is like is one of those things that we often have a picture in our head before we experience it.
            - What were your ideas about college before you came to this program?
            - In what ways have these ideas changed since being here?
        - Many of us also carry around a picture of who we are and what we are capable of doing. How has that picture changed for you while at the Precollege Scholarship Program?
        - What particular ways of thinking or specific skills did you take away from this experience?
        - Tell me about a time when you used this particular skill.
        - Say you are talking with a friend about your experience here, what are one or two things that you would tell them about your experience?
        - We will be doing this program again next summer. Is there anything else that you think we should know about the program?

THANK YOU!

Figure 8.1 Model group interview schedule.

Research exercise 8.1: Developing a group interview schedule

The first step in developing a group interview is to ask the "who" and "what" questions, i.e. "who do you want to interview?" and "what do you want to interview them about?" Group interviews are often good for gaining a sense of how a number of people responded to a particular experience that they shared in common. Assume that a large lecture class was exposed to a new method of teaching, say a lecture that used a small video clip to support a specific point and the use of computer coordinated clickers that were used to signal the instructor when someone did not understand an important point of concept in the lecture. You have been assigned to get some feedback for the instructor on how this new approach to lectures has influenced the students' attitude toward the class and the instructor's effectiveness. Using the example of a group interview above, construct a group interview schedule.

Be sure to include the mechanics of the group interview (Introduction and Consent) as illustrated in the example. The first challenge is to write a focus of inquiry. One important point to keep in mind is that the people whom you are interviewing may be considered as co-researchers. That is, they have the answers you are looking for. So the approach, unlike a traditional social psychology experiment, is not to fool the group that they are doing something other than what your focus of inquiry is. On the other hand, you do not want to lead them to respond in a way that you would like them to respond. Your focus needs to be open-ended. That's why the focus of inquiry often begins with "We would like to find out more about ..." The first question, in particular, should allow the interviewee to set the agenda for the discussion. Again, a more-or-less standard first question is "What stands out for you regarding ..." This keeps the focus on the topic while not leading the group in any predetermined direction. After the first open-ended question the group will have set the agenda, but there are things that you want to know, so unless you have much experience with group interviews and a command of the topic of inquiry, you need follow-up questions at the ready. A rule of thumb for these follow-up questions is to start with general questions and move to specific and more-narrow questions.

As with the individual semi-structured interview it is important to end by asking if there are other questions that might have been asked. This is not merely a polite thing to do, as that inquiry may lead to an extended discussion that the researcher had not anticipated. With a group interview this approach also encourages those who have not been active in the discussion to make a contribution. Minority opinions are highly valued.

Observation

Observing interaction in a classroom, a playground, or a clinic may be a valuable source of data. Any observations should take place over an extended period of time. By this I mean that a single observation ideally extends over a one-hour period and the observations should also occur on more than one occasion. The observer should be as unobtrusive as possible and to the extent possible act as a participant observer; that is, if appropriate, engage in the same activities as the group being observed. Notes are taken immediately after the observation and should include a diagram of the observation site, any quotes that can be remembered in a more-or-less exact manner, and the sequence of the interactions. Video and audio recordings are an alternative to participant observation and, if conducted in a relatively unobtrusive manner and with the consent of the participants, are a valuable data source. My experience is that if the equipment is minimal and the recording takes place over a regular interval (once a week, for example) the participants act "naturally" during the recording sessions.

Quantitative measures

Observation

Observation is also a data collection method in quantitative studies. Westerman (2006) provides a framework for quantitative observations. He suggests that inquirers take as their starting point that the behaviors being observed are a part of ongoing activities. "As such, the significance of a behavior depends on the role it plays in what the person is doing. Also, it is important to examine how it dovetails (i.e. meshes) with other behaviors to yield that activity" (Westerman 2006: 205). How that is done is by contextualizing the behaviors that we count. Westerman calls these processes relational codes. The point is to find ways to note not just what one person is saying or doing but how the comments and behaviors of the person involved mesh or fail to mesh with the other person's behaviors and words.

Surveys

Quantitative surveys that fit into the interpretative orientation work to capture a sense of process. An interpretative survey is likely to be given on more than one occasion, thus implying movement of ideas, the possibilities of changes in thinking. This orientation is in contrast to the typical survey that takes a snapshot of a person's thinking on the topic under investigation and assumes that it is a rather permanent position of the person over time and under all circumstances. Interpretative surveys should be sensitive to changes over time and in different environments. Sammons *et al.*'s (2007) work on teachers' work and lives and their effects on pupils provides a good example of effective use of surveys over time.

Experiments

Again turning to Michael Westerman's 2006 article, one way that an interpretative inquirer should look at experiments is as concrete examples of how one part of a practical activity influences another part of an activity (p. 206). In looking at practical activities, the usual practice of selecting independent variables needs to be thought of in a different light. The problem regarding independent variables for an interpretative inquiry project is that the goal is to make those variables so different from previous experiments that the variable becomes "independent" of life as an ongoing experience. It becomes isolated, and without context – other than being a part of an experiment. To counter this isolation, Westerman suggests, "experiments can be devised as environments in which the subject is truly involved in doing something so that the manipulation occurs in the context of that activity" (Westerman 2006: 207).

With an overview of some of the potential data collection tools you might use in your study, it is now time to provide a checklist of some issues to be reviewed before collecting any information. At Figure 8.2, in checklist format, is a set of prompts as you think about beginning your project. This checklist is derived from my work on several recent inquiry projects. I have found such a checklist helpful both as a planning framework as well as for a last review before launching an inquiry or evaluation.

Things to measure
    Knowledge ☐
        Product of change ☐
        Process of change ☐

    Attitudes ☐
        Interpersonal ☐
        Intrapersonal ☐
            Product of change ☐
            Process of change ☐
    Relationships ☐
        Interpersonal ☐
        Intrapersonal ☐
            Product of change ☐
            Process of change ☐

Ways to measure
    Measurement instruments ☐
        Paper and pencil instrument already available ☐
        Paper and pencil instrument to be created or modified ☐
    One-on-one in-depth interviews ☐
    Participant observation ☐
    Group interviews ☐

Who to measure
    All participants ☐
    Selected participants ☐

When to measure
    Before and after the project ☐
    Only after the project
    On-going data collection ☐
    Time specific data collection ☐

Figure 8.2 Checklist for planning and review of plans.

Data collection and data analysis go hand-in-hand. In a "purely" qualitative project, researchers often state that data analysis begins early and is ongoing. This is part of the emergent nature of a qualitative project. If one's data is exclusively quantitative, data analysis usually comes after all the data is collected. With a mixed method design the timing of data analysis is often early and ongoing for the qualitative data and at the end of data collection for the quantitative elements of the data.

Mixed methods measures

The key to collecting data for a mixed methods study is to collect similar or complementary data in similar timeframes and stay focused on understanding and action. A mixed methods data collection should create a more holistic understanding of the phenomenon under study. Counting or quantifying does not necessarily distance the inquirer and the eventual reader from accessing action and meaning. Michael Westerman (2006) argues that Likert-type scales and self-reports are interpretative instruments that may be used in conjunction with qualitative data. Instruments that purport to be objective measures of anxiety and abstract reasoning may also be used in conjunction with qualitative data so long as they contribute to a textual understanding of an activity and are not taken to be a definitive and permanent definition of a person. Participant observations, audio and video recordings as well as relevant documents may be helpful along with the quantitative data to aid an inquirer in forming a more or less holistic understanding of a phenomenon.

A comprehensive study of teachers' work, lives and their effects on pupils (Sammons *et al.* 2007) provides a model of such a study. This study "brought together research in two areas: mainly quantitative research on teacher (and school) effectiveness on the one hand and mainly qualitative research on teachers' work and lives on the other" (p. 683). The researchers used face-to-face interviews with teachers to assess what they called perceived effectiveness and used statistical information on pupils' progress as measured by the National Curriculum results to measure what they called relative effectiveness. This data was contextualized with information on the social economic status of pupils and schools, and experiences and education of teachers. Their goals, in part, were to "integrate different perspectives in order to better address the central questions" (p. 682) regarding teacher effectiveness from year to year and with experience, while examining biography and identity issues of teachers and social economic status and previous achievement level of pupils.

One of the keys to mixed method inquiries is to keep in mind the creation of a holistic understanding of persons in action. The focus is on understanding the perspectives of the individuals within specific contexts, rather than in establishing a fixed determination of a person or a phenomenon.

Data analysis

The goal of interpretative data analysis is to provide a way of simplifying without discarding complexity. The variability of human activity, and analysis of the patterns of stability and order within variation, are the elements that need to be simplified. Interpretative inquiry strives to understand the constructive, dynamic, and culturally embedded ways that people act as well as the organization or pattern of activities. The task of interpretative inquiry is to detect and describe patterns of variability and to propose models to account for data patterns that reflect both stability and variability.

In an interpretative inquiry, human activity is not seen as a static state of consciousness, or as idealized logical concepts, or other fixed forms but, as in the study of ecology, the analysis begins *in medias res*, that is, in the middle of things. To start in the middle of things means that people's activities are embodied, contextualized, and socially situated. We understand people and events in terms of their ecology as well as their structure. People act and understand through their bodies. While we may appear to act as individuals, our action is always taken jointly with other people (Fischer and Bidwell 1998: 468)

For Fischer and Bidwell (1998), the important analytical question is how the identity of the self or other is made relevant or attributed rather than whether or not it may be described in a particular way. In line with the concepts of identity outlined so far, the social psychologists Antaki and Widdicombe (1998) emphasize with their concept of "identities-in-interaction" the importance of discourse and interaction in the study of identities.

Types of data analysis or way of analyzing data

Qualitative data analysis

All qualitative data analysis begins with the verbatim transcription of any audio and video recorded materials. It is important to record as exactly as possible what the participants have said as qualitative inquiry is about capturing people's words and actions as a part of meaning-making. Some researchers are able to afford to have the transcripts professionally transcribed. A professional transcriber can complete the task more quickly than most researchers. This is a great advantage in saving time and energy. However, I encourage those new to the use of transcripts in research to transcribe some or all of the material themselves. While this effort takes a considerable amount of time (six to ten hours per hour of audio recording), it has the advantage of getting the inquirer very familiar with the data. When the researcher herself transcribes the interviews, she also gains a deeper and richer understanding of the information given by the inquiry participant.

Transcription of auditory or visual recording begins the process of analysis. This is a time-consuming process. A transcript is a verbatim record of an individual or group interview. Each transcript has an identification code placed in the header on the top of each page. The code identifies the transcript according to salient characteristics. An individual interview transcript may be organized as follows: interviewer's initial for first name, interviewee's initial for first name, and time of interview plus the page number of the transcript. If the interviewer is Richard and he is interviewing Mary on July 10, 2011 and this is the first page of the interview the code would look like this: R-M-7-10-11 #1. The codes may be of your own creation but it is essential that you have a separate sheet of paper that has the details of the code. Codes vary with the type of transcript. For example, in a project I conducted with a group of undergraduate students we video-recorded a series of tutoring sessions. The research team developed a code that identifies the tutor and the date the session was recorded.

Once the transcription is completed, the next task is to parse, or divide, the transcripts – forming the raw qualitative data – into units of meaning. A unit of meaning is a complete idea or concept or interaction. Units of meaning are hard to define and to delimit. Hinde's discussion of interaction or encounter may be used to help determine the perimeters of a unit of meaning.

> By an "interaction" or "encounter" in Goffman's (1961; 1963) terminology – we mean such incidence as individual A shows behavior X and individual B responds with Y. Of course most interactions are longer than this, but the question of how long a series of social interactions can be and still qualify as a single need not detain us. Clearly there is no absolute answer, and any discussion must be based on what is empirically useful.
>
> (Hinde 1997: 36)

Another way to circumscribe a unit of meaning is to ask if the ideas can more-or-less provide meaning for a person who has a limited understanding of the larger context of the study. Each unit of meaning is cut from the transcript and taped to a 5 × 6 index card. A complete uncut transcript should be maintained. This is important as the researcher may need to go back to the original transcript to check the context of the statement. The inquirer may also wish to reread the entire transcript or portions of it to keep that narrative flow of the interview or video-recorded session in mind.

Discovery is the inquirer's next task. This involves listing, based on the inquirer's knowledge of the data, several potential important concepts or ideas thought to be in the transcripts. Working in a team or individually, list a number of key ideas or concepts on a white board or computer screen. Seven to ten ideas will do for a start. As the inquirers have immersed themselves in the data via transcript analysis, they will have a good sense of important concepts. If the researcher has not transcribed his own transcripts, it is essential to carefully read all the transcripts before beginning. One way to simultaneously gain a deep sense of the data and expedite the completion of the transcripts is to use a jigsaw approach. The jigsaw approach works like this: each inquirer transcribes an interview they conducted plus one other interview. The interview that they did not do is compared with the interview done by another member of the research team. Any discrepancies are resolved by first reviewing the audio or visual recording and then by examining the perspective of the person who conducted the interview. Another version of the jigsaw transcription process when transcribing video sessions that are not interviews works like this. An instructor and a group of five student researchers collected video recordings of sessions with undergraduate tutors and tutees. Each researcher completed two transcripts, and then reviewed two transcripts completed by two other students. The video record was consulted to resolve any discrepancies.

With the discoveries posted in place for all to see, the process of placing units of meaning into categories begins. Using the discovery statement for beginning categories, the researcher now begins placing the unitized cards into the discovery categories. Maykut and Morehouse (1994) called the inclusion strategy "looks like/feels like." The strategy works like this. If a card (unit of meaning) looks like and feels like the discovery category place the card in that category. If it does not fit into one of the discovery categories, start a new category using that card as the first card in the category. The placing of cards into categories and all subsequent data analysis is best done publically and aloud. Even projects that are primarily conducted by one person might consider working with an assistant at this phase of the project.

After there are four or five cards in a category, stop the process of putting up cards and make a rule for inclusion. A rule for inclusion states in a declarative sentence the nature of the category. Another sentence may be added to clarify what does not belong in the category. All units of meaning will eventually find their way into a category. All the data, that is, units of meaning, should eventually find their way into a category.

The data analysis I use when teaching is very visually oriented. I recommend it for all beginning qualitative researchers. A visual approach begins by putting up the data on a wall so that all the people working on the project can see it. While there are computer generated programs that work for doing qualitative data analysis, it is helpful, especially for those new to research, to get as close to the data as possible. When all of the cards are placed into a category this phase of the process is completed. Some cards may be in a category called "miscellaneous." These items do not fit into a category other than miscellaneous but should be kept track of in case they might be useful later; the point is to not discard any data no matter how unimportant it may appear at the time.

To summarize this process, placing the units of meaning into thematic categories is the essence of the constant comparative method. It begins by creating inductive categories and comparing each unit of meaning across all the categories. During that process categories are refined and rules for inclusions are developed. Relationships between categories or patterns across categories are also arrived at inductively. For a detailed account of this process see Maykut and Morehouse, 1994, Chapter 9. An approach to using Microsoft Word as a tool for data analysis is presented in Appendix A.

My experience has been that it is the data analysis phase that gets the inquirer excited about research. To begin to see patterns emerge from the data often generates an enthusiasm in the researchers, and especially in those new to the process of qualitative data analysis. An anecdote will illustrate this experience. While a group of student researchers and I were working on the data analysis for the epigenetic study of tutoring (Morehouse *et al.* 2010) a colleague walked into the research room in the midst of our placing units of meaning into categories. The colleague observed the process for about five to seven minutes and then left the room. The student researchers were so involved that none of them noticed his presence.

With all of the units of meaning placed into categories and rules written for each category, the next task is to group the categories into larger themes. A theme may be seen as a device to move the individual bit of information into a narrative. A somewhat different way of thinking about themes is as vignettes or a short evocative descriptions. After reading all the categories into which you have placed the units of meaning, group together all of the categories that seem to go together. Now write a theme statement or a vignette that captures how these categories form a new whole. This new whole becomes your theme. For each theme pick a number of direct quotes that illustrate the theme. These will become the core element of the narrative for the writing of the final paper for publication to be presented in Chapter 10.

Quantitative

Data analysis from an interpretative perspective uses as its beginning place a person who is doing something and whose activities are connected with the activities of others; these activities are in a context and "dovetail" with the activities of others (Westerman 2006: 104). "The key point here is that even though mathematics is used via data analysis, our explanation of phenomena is not mathematical in nature. ... because the mathematical aspects are embedded in a larger context of meaningful interpretative procedures" (Westerman 2006: 194). As a practical matter this means that whatever statistical procedure is used to analyze that data, the inquirer needs to make clear that she is working to make meaning, to make sense of the findings by using a mathematical procedure to illustrate some activity within a larger context than a mere response to some stimuli and this context meshes or dovetails with the actions of others.

Data analysis for a mixed method inquiry

In some ways there is nothing new about data analysis with a mixed methods inquiry if the focus is narrowly on analysis. However, as interpretation is a part of analysis, the way the data is presented and interpreted is important. Steven Yanchar and David Williams' work on establishing criteria for mixed methods research provides a perspective on what interpretative inquirers' using mixed methods need to pay attention to. Yanchar and Williams begin their guidelines for mixed methods inquiry by emphasizing that the problem being studied, the questions being asked, and the tools being used to find answers need to be compatible. This means that as a part of the data analysis the inquirer ought to make clear how the quantitative methods support the qualitative methods and vice versa, and this means more than placing the results next to each other. What is required in order to make the different sources of data and the different methods of collecting that data into a coherent whole is to articulate the manner in which one data set informs the other data set. It may seem obvious, but that means looking carefully to see the extent to which the data sets address similar questions in similar contexts (Yanchar and Williams 2006: 9).

Summary

By placing data collection and data analysis in the same chapter, my purpose was to draw attention to the continuity of the two processes. New researchers are likely to get caught up in the excitement of data collection and overlook data analysis when planning the data collection phase. If, during the data collection planning, the inquirer is also thinking about data analysis, some potential problems may be solved. As we will see in Chapter 10, the methods section of the writing of the project includes data collection methods as well as data analysis methods. The two processes are not placed together primarily for the ease of writing a project, but because the two processes are, or ought to be, nearly seamless.

Perhaps this is an appropriate time to reflect on the integration of the entire planning process and its relationship to the writing of the findings of the inquiry. The two processes, planning the inquiry project and writing the findings of the inquiry, are reverse sides of the same process. While the planning process is conceptualized as a step-by-step process, the process in practice is more organic. The trick is to keep the whole in mind as you develop the details and to let the details inform the whole as the process moves forward. As will become clear in Chapter 9, this whole/part back and forth process will also be true for the writing.

However, before beginning to write the results of an inquiry and preparing a manuscript for publication, inquirers need to consider some of the ethical issues involved in all research and evaluation projects. While researchers and evaluators need to be aware of ethical issues from the beginning of their projects, I have placed the ethical considerations in Chapter 9 as it is integral to proposal writing. The Institutional Review of your project provides an opportunity to rethink the whole of your project and it also prepares you for the writing of your findings.

Ethics and the Institutional Review Board (IRB)

All researchers and evaluators need to address issues of ethics when conducting a research or evaluation project. The legal requirements are limited to research projects; however, the requirements presented in an IRB are helpful guidelines for evaluation projects. When writing an inquiry proposal, ethical issues of data collection and dissemination need to be addressed. The project proposal must be submitted to the Institutional Review Board (IRB) before data collection can begin. Institutional Review Boards are also known as an independent ethics committee (IEC) or ethical review board (ERB). In the United Kingdom, the ERB review levels are Department Ethics Committee (DEC) for most routine research; Institutional Ethics Committee (IEC) for non-routine research; and External Ethics Committee (EEC) for research that is externally regulated (British Psychological Society 2004: 6). These levels roughly match with the IRB levels in the United States discussed above.

The American Educational Research Association states that a study approval in accordance with an IRB should be stated (AERA 2006). The IRB process aids the researcher in addressing ethical issues and in many ways helps the inquirer during the final stage of proposal writing. New inquirers sometimes see this step as a hurdle to getting on with the research or evaluation project. My sense is that while the review process may slow down the beginning of the project it will aid the inquirer by improving the project or at the very least provide assurance that important ethical issues have been properly addressed.

The IRB is responsible for the well-being and safety of the participants in the study. In the United States, IRBs are governed by Title 45 CFR (Code of Federal Regulations) Part 46, section 1. These regulations implement provisions of the National Research Act of 1974. As a general rule, all research that is funded by a government agency requires the funded institution to have an Institutional Review Board. The board is also a guardian of the rights of study participants. Informed consent of the participants is one of the important concerns attended to in the IRB process. The board is also concerned with balancing risks to participants in the study and benefits to the society. Vulnerable subjects, such as pregnant women, minor children, prisoners, the elderly, and persons of limited cognitive abilities, are specified as populations that require careful consideration before the study is allowed to go forward.

There are three levels of review. The first level of review is called exempted. This is something of a misnomer as the proposal is submitted for review but not to the review board. The reviewer in academic settings is usually the department chair, or if the researcher is a department chair then the proposal is submitted to the person who oversees the work of the department chair. Projects where all the participants are adults, the intervention is routine, and the subjects are identified only as a group, generally fall within the exempted category.

The second level is expedited. This level requires a minimum review of some ethics committee members. Some institutions may require the full ethics committee to meet; however, the process is routine. The ethics board members read the proposal carefully to see if all the requirements concerning privacy, consent, and security of information are intact. Of special concern of the board is the risk to human subjects (study participants).

A full review procedure is required where identification of the subjects and/or their responses would reasonably place them at risk of criminal or civil liability or be damaging to the subjects' financial standing or reputation. The review board is also sensitive to any potential stigmatizing of participants. In any research that has the potential for participants to be identified, the review board requires the implementation of safeguards to limit risks of invasion of privacy and breach of confidentiality to a minimum.

The exempted form includes a cover sheet with information such as the title of the project, the name of the primary investigator and all other investigators, contact information such as phone numbers and addresses. This identifying information is followed by questions regarding the study. The questionnaire includes questions regarding how the study is conducted, whether the study participants can be identified (directly or indirectly), if there are any sensitive aspects of the participants' behavior that will be examined, if the participants are 18 years of age or older, and other similar questions. A more detailed form usually follows. This form contains questions on the nature of the procedures or activities the participants will undergo, whether any vulnerable populations are involved in the study, how the participants will be informed regarding their rights, what will be done to ensure the anonymity of the participants, and an assessment of the extent to which the study contributes to the knowledge of the participants and to the body of knowledge.

Informed consent is an important part of the IRB. Participants are required to give their permission to be a part of study or evaluation (Viterbo University, n.d.). This agreement must be given freely and be an informed choice. Find a completed informed consent form in Appendix B. It is an example of an informed consent form taken from a research project a colleague and I conducted with students in an undergraduate research class.

Research exercise 9.1: Informed consent

Using the project that you have been working on and the model for an informed consent in Appendix B, write your own consent form. Be sure to make it clear to the participants that they are free to engage in the project and that they can withdraw at any time without penalty and that their choosing to withdraw from the project will not affect the project.

Check your final Informed Consent Form against the model one in Appendix B. The language in the model is only an example, so you should not repeat the wording verbatim but put things in your own words. It is important that your wording matches the knowledge and experience of the study participants. Do not talk (write) down to the participants. Likewise, you need to be sure that the participants understand the nature of the project and any potential risks to them. They also should know the potential benefits of the project, and how they will be informed about the results of the inquiry.

With the approval of the ethics board the research is ready to begin. Ethical considerations, however, also include the writing of the final report or the manuscript to be submitted for publication. The reporting of one's data should be consistent with what the researcher set out in her informed consent agreement and all other parts of the IRB. The ability to keep the identity of the participants confidential in the presentation of the results is paramount.

Conflict of interest should be avoided. If a potential conflict exists, it needs to be clearly identified as well as the manner in which the researcher addressed the conflict. Funding sources should be identified. Finally, the essential data that would be required for a qualified researcher to check the veracity of your findings should be saved if your findings are challenged (AREA 2006: 39–40). For a qualitative project this means saving all the original documents and transcripts as well as notes about decision-making that provide an audit trail. For a quantitative study one needs to maintain copies of the original instruments as marked by participants as well as statistical programs used in the analysis of the data. Mixed methods projects need to maintain both types of information.

Chapter 10

Writing for publication

All inquiry projects are intended for publication of some sort. Writing for dissemination is the final stage of a research or evaluation project. At the beginning of the project the inquirers most likely thought that the questions they raised, the issues they addressed, and the methods they applied in the project were important for a larger audience. The writing of the project is the test of ideas regarding questions, issues, and methods which will now be offered for scrutiny by some anonymous persons outside the immediate circle of the inquirers. Even a small project ought to be disseminated. But it is equally true that most inquiry projects will not be published as articles in juried journals. However, there are many other venues for dissemination of an inquiry project.

I begin by discussing the formats and criteria for submission of these venues. Evaluation projects, unlike research projects, have an immediate and obvious audience, i.e. a report to the person or agency who commissioned the evaluation. I will discuss the writing of an evaluation project later in this chapter as many of the concerns about an evaluation project report will be addressed as we look to the writing and public presentation of the inquiry findings. I will also explore some of the ways in which evaluation projects can reach larger audiences by modifying the evaluation report for submission to a peer reviewed journal.

From inquiry finding to publication

I begin with a short description of each of the venues for the dissemination of research and how the review process works. The presentation of these venues is ordered by the standards for inclusion from most exclusive to most inclusive. The most rigorous standards, and therefore the most exclusive venues, are those of the juried journal. The least rigorous standards are those of the local conference. This is not to say that local and regional conferences are not of value, only that they are more likely to accept research that has a smaller number of participants in the study, and perhaps they will accept studies that are a little more tentative and less robust in their results. All submissions need to be well written and the studies need to be well designed and carefully executed.

A journal article is a peer-reviewed manuscript that has been accepted for publication. The journal article is the pinnacle of the presentation pyramid in that it is highly regarded and exclusive as most research is disseminated at conferences and does not find its way to journals. The format of journal articles is already familiar to beginning inquirers as they have immersed themselves in reading in order to write a research or evaluation proposal. The journal article will be discussed first and in greatest detail, as the other platforms are derivations of the journal article. The goal of all inquiry is to communicate one's findings and peer-reviewed journal articles are the standard venue for almost all research. The review process is blind and anonymous.

Briefly, the process works like this. A journal editor receives your article, usually electronically. The editor, after initial examination of the manuscript, sends the author a reply saying that the manuscript was received and indicates that it has been sent out for review. A time frame for the review process will often be included with this email response. The editor, relying first on consulting editors and/or the editorial board (most likely listed in the opening pages of the journal), finds two or three persons with expertise in the topic of the paper to serve as potential reviewers. The editor invites the jurors to consider reviewing the article usually by sending the reviewer a copy of the article abstract. The journal editor may also ask the consulting editors and board members to suggest potential additional reviewers. If the potential reviewer agrees to review the article, he or she will receive a copy of the manuscript with all identification of the author removed. This is what makes the review "blind" in that the reviewer does not know who submitted the manuscript. It is also anonymous in that only the editor, and not the author of the manuscript, knows who the reviewer is. Reviewers are asked to assess the appropriateness of the article for this particular journal and the acceptability of the article as a scholarly inquiry. The reviewers comment on the strengths and weaknesses of the article, the rationale for the study, the contribution of the study to the specific field of inquiry, and the logic of the study, including research methods and data analysis. Finally, the reviewers are asked to accept the article (as is or with minor revisions), accept with major revisions, or to reject the article for publication in this journal. If an article is accepted with major revisions, the editor often recommends that the manuscript be resubmitted to the original reviewers along with the reviewers' original comments. In some cases, the reviewer will also receive the comments of other reviewers of the original manuscript. This allows the reviewers to make a decision on the acceptance of the manuscript based on the perspective of the other reviewers. This not only allows for confirmation of similar criticisms but also for disagreement, thus allowing the editor to weigh the pros and cons of the reviewers' comments on the resubmitted manuscript.

Conference papers are very similar to journal articles in their format and style. The submission process is also similar in that the review is blind and anonymous. The differences are important. While a journal editor has time to select reviewers and the person or team submitting the manuscript is given the opportunity to improve the paper as a part of the acceptance process, conference papers are generally accepted or rejected. On occasion a paper may be recommended for submission to next year's conference, but some conferences are organized around themes and the paper may not fit with new conference theme.

The presentation of a conference paper generally follows a similar pattern. Conference papers are often grouped with three to four other papers. Two other people often share the platform or dais with the presenters: a person to introduce the topic and the presenters, and a discussant. The discussant reads all the papers before the conference and performs two tasks during the conference. First she comments on each of the papers pointing to strengths, contributions, and weaknesses of the individual paper. The discussant follows the comments on individual papers by making connections between the papers pointing out similarities and differences in themes, outcomes, and approaches. After the discussant completes her prepared comments, the floor is open to questions by the audience.

Posters are a more informal way to present inquiry findings. A poster is a short version of a full-length research paper usually restricted by the number of words (abstract 300 words or fewer) and the recommended point size and typeface for viewing at three feet (27 point type). It includes an abstract, an introduction including the problem statement and research question, a methods section, results, and references. It is displayed on a large sheet of poster board. Generally, posters are 4 feet (122 cm) tall and six feet (183 cm) wide. Many conference organizers also asked that the poster presenters bring with them 25 to 50 copies of the full paper available for anyone who asks for one. The poster format allows hundreds of conference attendees to file past a series of posters with a quick glance to see if the topic is of interest to them. If it is, they will often engage the poster presenter or presenters in questions about the research, often taking a copy of the full paper to read at a later time. Posters provide a potential egalitarian engagement between new scholars and veterans. If the presenter(s) are new researchers, veteran researchers often stop to offer support and gentle criticism. On the other hand, if the presenter is an established scholar, new researchers find the informal setting gives them an opportunity to engage the senior scholar with questions that they might not normally feel comfortable in asking, for example, in a large conference hall with hundreds of other scholars.

Roundtables are a relative newcomer to national and international conferences. A roundtable is a conversation around a table sometimes with a working draft of a paper. Graduate students on occasion use this format to talk about ongoing research. Ten to twelve people including the presenter, after a short presentation about the topic, sit and talk about the project at hand and also about the work that each of them is doing. While the person convening the roundtable may have a more formal paper, the point is to engage in a conversation about a topic of mutual interest. Roundtables are accepted or rejected by peer review panels the same as other conference presentations. The criteria for review are specific to the conference. A created example of the criteria for a roundtable will be presented later in this chapter.

Preparing an article for a juried journal

The outline presented here is linear, moving from step-to-step. This organization is for pedagogic reasons, in practice there will be more flexibility in terms of the specific ordering of the steps, however, each of the steps is essential regardless of their order. At the end of this section I will comment on some of the cases where the steps might be modified.

All manuscripts, quantitative, qualitative, and mixed method manuscripts, should begin with a clear statement of the problem that situates that problem within a larger context, explains why it is important to the reader of the selected journal, and outlines the manner in which the researcher intends to address the problem. This includes a review of the relevant literature, that is, the past research as well as the theoretical background that applies to the topic at hand. Some sense of the theoretical landscape of your project is important as it helps to illustrate the importance and relevance of the inquiry problem. This information is followed by the design and the logic of your inquiry project. The logic of the study allows the reader to follow the path of your inquiry (AERA 2006: 34). The design statement tells the reader of an interpretative study how particular occurrences and the meanings people give them are to be gathered and analyzed.

A few words on citation are in order as one prepares to write for publication. All juried journals have a preferred publication style. Most journals use some version of the citation and reference format of the APA style manual (2009a, 2009b). The generic name for an APA-like citation style is often called Harvard citation and referencing style. The Harvard style, as best as I can determine from examining a number of journal submission guidelines, is a system of citation that provides the reader with information regarding the author, date of publication and page number for a direct quote or close paraphrase within the text of the article. This information is enclosed in parentheses. Specifics of the house version of the Harvard style are generally stated in some detail in a section in the journal on how to submit. At the end of the article a complete list of all citations are presented in alphabetical order under the heading of references or works cited. Because many journals have specific modifications of the generic Harvard citation method and the journal that one plans to submit to may not be determined until the manuscript is completed, I recommend that new inquirers use the APA style manual (2009a, 2009b) in the initial preparation of their research. Using the APA style guidelines has several advantages. First, the APA style is used quite widely beyond the APA's journal. Second, in submitting for most publications, the author will have to make only minor modifications to comply with the selected journal's citation and referencing guidelines. Third, the APA style manual is readily accessible in two book forms, the full manual (APA 2009a) and a *Concise Guide* (APA 2009b) and there is online advice from the Purdue Online Writing Lab (2010) that is available free of charge.

When writing a juried article for publication the title page may be more important than it appears when submitting a research paper for a university course. The title page allows the editor to keep track of the essential information regarding the manuscript. This page is removed when the manuscript is distributed to the reviewers who will decide on the publication value of the manuscript. The title page contains a title in upper and lower case and is centered both from left to right and from top to bottom. Under the title are the author's name or names and the institutional affiliation. The words "running head" followed by a colon, then a space, then the short title of the paper in all capital letters. This is placed on the upper left hand of the page in the header. The page number is placed in the header on the right side of the page. The page number function from a word processing program should be used, as the running head will be repeated throughout the length of the manuscript.

On a new page, following the title page, is the abstract. An empirical study, regardless of the data collection methods used, should begin with an abstract of 300 words or fewer. The abstract is intended to provide the reader of the journal with the key elements of the article including the method for data collection and analysis and the most important findings. Some journals may also ask for key words to be included at the end of the manuscript abstract. Key words are used in database search engines to find the article. The body of the manuscript, which begins a new page, follows the abstract.

All empirical studies should include a review of the relevant scholarship that bears directly on the topic of the report. In most cases the review section begins with a presentation of how the search was conducted: what databases were consulted, what key words were used in the search and the years that framed the boundaries. This section of the paper is not usually given a heading. The review goes on to provide the reader with the criteria used to identify and select the relevant scholarship that grounds the study. The review provides a clear picture of how the study contributes to, challenges, and/or extends theory, practice, methodology, research results, knowledge and/or understandings within an area of inquiry (AERA 2006). As the review of the literature is for an interpretative inquiry, it is more likely than not to include at least some qualitative studies. With the inclusion of qualitative, quantitative, and mixed methods studies comes the responsibility to provide a theoretical perspective on how these studies can be integrated and understood as making a contribution to the topic at hand. The review of the literature also includes some of the literature that contextualizes the study in terms of the historical, linguistic, social, and cultural backgrounds of the group. The review of the literature ends with a restatement of the research problem.

There are differences between quantitative, qualitative, and mixed methods manuscripts. I begin by presenting the organization for quantitative articles.

Quantitative studies

Following the review of the literature is a presentation of the research methods in the study. This section begins with the word "Methods." This section presents the conceptual, methodological, and sometimes the theoretical characteristics of the study. Specifically the number of subjects in the study and how they were selected should be included. The instruments used in the data collection and some comment about their validity and reliability is also included. There should also be a statement regarding the design of the study. A transition sentence connects the Methods section with the Results section.

The results are presented next. This section begins with the heading "Results." The initial statement in the narrative section is a summary of the most important findings. Somewhat counter-intuitively, it helps to prepare any statistical table that you plan to use before you write this section. You may not end up using any of the tables that you prepared, but having all the information in condensed form will make the writing easier. After the big picture of your research is presented, go into as much detail regarding the statistics as seem necessary. Do not present the entire array of statistics that you have. Generally present descriptive statistics before inferential statistics. Use tables and charts only when these methods of presentation make a point that cannot easily be made with a written statement.

The Discussion section provides the interpretation and evaluation of the results. A smooth transition between these two sections is created by a brief, non-technical summary of the results that informs the reader. The discussion is in some ways a continuation of the results section but also thoughtfully contextualizes to connect to the review of the literature. It ties together the results with the review of the literature. It is important to relate the findings back to the theoretical, content, and methodological issues presented in the review of the literature. As the focus here is on interpretative studies, be sure to keep in mind that the study privileges action, agency, and meaning-making. This section generally includes the inquirer's perspective on what research is left undone on this topic. The Discussion ends with a restatement of the findings that the inquirer has drawn from the study and places the research within a contextual framework. The American Educational Research Association provides a very helpful guide for conducting and writing results for quantitative studies (AERA 2006).

Qualitative studies

The guidelines for a manuscript for a qualitative inquiry are not as well established as those for a quantitative study. The title page and the abstract follow the same format and construction as quantitative inquiries. The organization of the other sections is different in an important way. To begin with, the format may include somewhat different headings for each of the sections.

I will present a generic model, in lieu of a standard model, that may be modified to fit the parameters of most journals that accept qualitative studies. The qualitative manuscript usually begins with an introduction, sometimes with a heading as such and sometimes without any heading. The introduction defines the problem being studied and elaborates on the value of a qualitative approach to the problem. This will provide a lead into the review of the literature and provide the beginning of a structure for sorting out the use of quantitative, qualitative, and mixed method inquiries.

The next section is the review of the literature. Like the quantitative review, it begins with a presentation of how the search was conducted. However, unlike a typical quantitative study, a qualitative study is likely to include a theoretical framework for the study as well as a general review of the literature. Additionally, in presenting findings from the review of previous inquiries, it is important to clarify whether the cited sources used quantitative, qualitative, or mixed methods of data collection as analysis. This is important, as one of the goals of the review is to place the reviewed studies within an interpretative framework. Some quantitative studies may be on the positivist end of the spectrum and therefore will not make a suitable contribution to understanding within an interpretative framework. On the other hand, a positivist study may be used to indicate why the direction taken in the interpretative study is important in understanding a particular phenomenon. The inclusion of the theoretical framework for the study is important, as it will set up a presentation of data collection and analysis in the Methods section.

In the generic model, this section is called Methods of Inquiry. As distinct from Methods, this section highlights the discovery approach endemic to most qualitative inquiries. The Methods of Inquiry section of the manuscript is of particular importance as it sets up the criteria for the trustworthiness and transferability of the study by focusing on the way the data in collected and analyzed. Also important to be included in this section is information on the site of the inquiry and the participants in the study. By elaborating on the site of the inquiry the researcher provides documentation for the reader regarding the context and limits of the research. Information on important characteristics of the participants also increases the reader's understanding of the context and limitations of the inquiry. This section is key to establishing the believability of the data and its interpretation. Some qualitative articles have an underdeveloped Methods of Inquiry section. This is a concern as it leads readers to think the qualitative methods are less than rigorous. Anyone who has conducted qualitative analysis knows the hard and careful work that goes into transcription, unitizing the data, and finding and confirming propositions and themes. A well-written method of inquiry section will help dispel the idea that the project they are reading is not rigorous.

Finding and Discussion are often included in one section in a qualitative manuscript as the themes that emerge from the data are framed within the context of the theoretical issues. The themes of the narrative emerge from the data supported by individual statements and documents. These themes are woven with threads from the data interwoven with theoretically based knowledge about the phenomenon. This will likely be the longest section of the manuscript as the richness and comprehensiveness of the data is what allows for the plausibility and authenticity of the narrative. It is important to find quotes that are long enough to capture important ideas that characterize key elements of the theme. Weaving a narrative with theoretical elements and specific quotes or action frames taken directly from the data is both art and science. The science derives from the careful analysis of the transcripts and documents; the art comes in creating a flowing narrative, based on a deep understanding of the issues that surround the topic, that tells the story contained in the data. Like the quantitative inquiries discussed earlier, the Finding and Discussion section connects back to the review of the literature. The Finding and Discussion section ends with a restatement of the findings within a theoretical perspective.

Mixed method studies

The format for mixed method interpretative studies may well be the least well established. *The Publication Manual of the American Psychological Association* (2009a) for example does not have any information on the format for a mixed method article or on qualitative articles. The American Educational Research Association has published guidelines for humanities-oriented research and for empirical social science research (AERA 2006, 2009). Both articles are useful to those working on interpretative projects. However, there is no information provided on how to write an article with mixed methods of data collection and analysis. Drawing from published articles using mixed methods, here is a way to write up results from an interpretative inquiry that uses mixed methods. AERA standards (AERA 2006, 2009) provide the major source suggestions for writing one's findings in an interpretative mixed method design.

Research exercise 10.1: Peer reviewing

As a quick exercise in peer review, choose an article of interest (or the manuscript you have been working on) and assess the article using the guidelines below. In completing this activity you may just check the box for each item or you may write a more complete statement. The point of the exercise is to become familiar with how reviewers look at the work of others, not to train you as a peer reviewer. However, as your career progresses you may well be asked to review the works of others.

Some journal editors also ask if the article might be appropriate for another journal. This would occur if the article were thought to be of scholarly merit but not necessarily appropriate for the journal to which it was submitted.

Title of article
Date published
Name, number of volume and issue, and page numbers for article
As a potential juror for this article how would you rate this article in the following categories?

- Contribution to field of knowledge
    Significant □   Not significant □
- Originality
    Highly original □   Moderately original □   Minimally original □
- Theoretical framework
    Well thought-out and well-argued □   Weakly thought-out and argued □
- Structure of the argument
    Well-framed □   Poorly framed □
- Substance of the argument
    Comprehensive □   Incomplete □
- Clarity of the writing
    Easily understood by a well-informed general reader □
    Full of unnecessary academic jargon □

- References
    - Complete and accurate ☐
- Abstract
    - Does the abstract preview the content of the article? ☐

- Accept or accept with minor revisions ☐
- Accept with major revisions ☐
- Reject ☐

To summarize, all research writing whether quantitative, qualitative, or mixed method investigations, should follow a clear logic of inquiry that allows readers to trace the path followed by the inquirer. This path begins with the initial statement of the problem, moves to a review of the literature and on to the research question. The next step is a description of the site and participants in the study. This is followed by an analysis of the data. The write-up ends with the presentation and interpretation of the data and the construction of a framework for understanding the contributions and limitations of the inquiry (AERA 2006: 34–35).

Posters

Posters are the most common format for young researchers. As a rule posters have a somewhat less rigorous standard for acceptance than do articles or formal papers at conferences. A poster is a way of presenting the findings of your inquiry project on a display board (poster) at a conference. The poster sessions are set up in large open spaces with room for conference attendees to read the results of the research or evaluation project. This allows the conference attendees to read and pass by, or read, stop, and ask questions.

A typical poster has one of several formats. Figure 10.1 shows one possible format. Conference calls for papers will have additional information of how to prepare a poster for that specific conference.

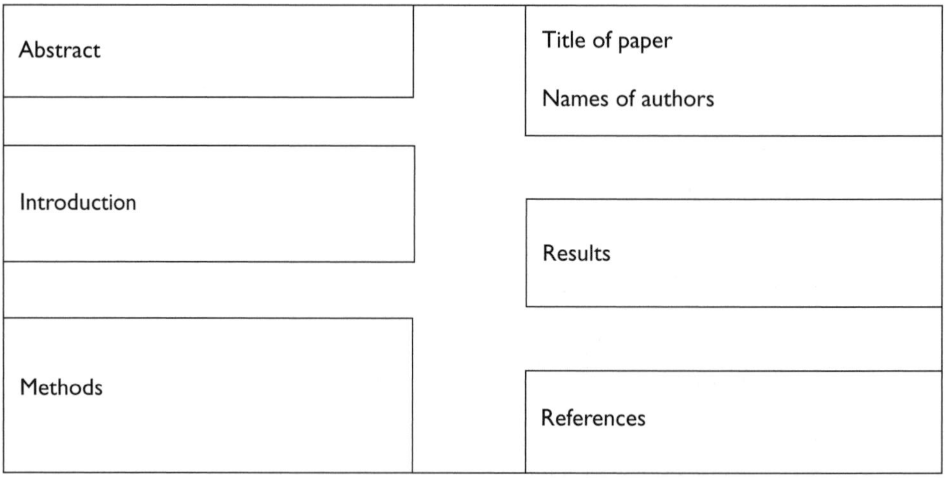

Abstract	Title of paper
	Names of authors
Introduction	
	Results
Methods	
	References

Figure 10.1 Poster design.

Roundtable presentation/discussion

The conference roundtable is most different from the other ways of making your ideas accessible to a larger scholarly audience so I will present it last. While some detail may differ from conference to conference, most roundtables share these characteristics:

1   they are informal ways for getting feedback,
2   they are small presentations usually restricted to twelve or fewer (just a large enough audience to sit around a large oval table),
3   the presenters are seeking feedback in order to improve the project, and
4   the orientation is more collegial, more dialogical than a formal paper presentation.

Even with these restrictions, you should have a working version of a paper or a very detailed outline in order to facilitate a discussion and get solid feedback.

To prepare for a roundtable discussion begin by outlining the major issue(s) to be discussed. An emerging or controversial topic is well suited for a roundtable discussion. If the emerging topic is drawn from your own experience or your own work the discussion will be livelier and your ability to manage the discussion will be greater. Begin with a short introduction to the topic of the session and highlight several issues to be covered in the discussion. Sometimes presenters use a laptop computer to present a PowerPoint with key discussion points. As an attendee at roundtables, I have found that a handout with an outline of key issues is equally effective. Roundtables are a good way to expand one's network of likeminded scholars as participants often exchange business cards with discussants who share a deep interest in the topic.

Appendix A

Introductory comments

The method of electronic data analysis was developed at Viterbo University by one student (Hailey Karls-Lange) and two faculty members. As the authors indicate in the description on how to conduct constant comparative qualitative data analysis, the electronic application came after the research team had already immersed themselves in a considerable amount of data and data analysis on the same topic with similar subjects. While I remain an advocate of old-fashioned hand-to-paper-on-the-wall analysis, there is a place for electronic data analysis if the researchers have considerable confidence in their ability to conduct data analysis from previous experience and if they take precautions to stay close to the data and not to let the process be taken over by the technology. I think that the processes outlined below keep the researchers close to the data and keep the intentions of the participants in the forefront.

An electronic way to conduct qualitative data analysis

Hailey Karls-Lange, Valerie J. Kokott-Rebhahn, and Debra A. Murray

After completion of a pilot study (started in the summer of 2009) entitled "Mapping the Future: Resiliency, Relational Development and Recovery" that involved qualitative data analysis (utilizing the constant comparative method) (Maykut and Morehouse 1994) of five women's stories with previous substance use disorders, the idea of making the analysis procedure electronic emerged. Another pilot study on the same topic started for five men during that same summer; however, data continued to be gathered for the men through the summer of 2010. After completion of gathering the data for the men in their pilot study, some issues prompted the need for and an exploration of an electronic data organization method.

The issues that prompted this need were as follows:

1   unitizing, cutting, and pasting verbatim transcriptions onto note cards was time consuming;
2   communication, processing, and time barriers occurred when the entire team could not meet all together in one room to analyze data;
3   there was limited wall space available for the full qualitative analysis process; and
4   if something were to happen to the transcribed, unitized, and organized data, there would be no backup document other than the raw transcription on the computer.

In response to these issues, a structural analysis method was developed that allows researchers to type verbatim transcriptions into a word document, unitize the data using Microsoft Word "comment" review system, and copy and paste the unitized data into appropriate themes. Because this method utilizes a Microsoft Office Word document, which many students, researchers, and professors commonly use, it is low cost (as it is installed on most academic computers), relatively easy to understand, and definitely helps with the physical space issue.

For the electronic method of data analysis to take place, researchers must have a standard Microsoft Office Word document installed on the computer that will allow researchers to manipulate data and view the analysis on a computer or larger projector screen. Additionally, the following is required before beginning to electronically organize data:

1   transcribe the interview verbatim into a Word document and identify the interviewer and research participant with code names.
2   unitize the data as would traditionally take place with the constant comparative method. In electronic analysis this is more easily done through "comments." Highlight the segment of text that represents a particular concept or idea to be unitized, click on "Review" in the Word toolbar, and click "New Comment." Type the identified concept along with the participant name, page number, and segment number. For example, "loss of a loved one; Henry 12-3" would signify that on page 12, the third concept identified was that Henry discussed the loss of a loved one.

When unitization is complete, save the file in a safe location, back it up (highly recommended), and refer back to it if needed later during analysis.

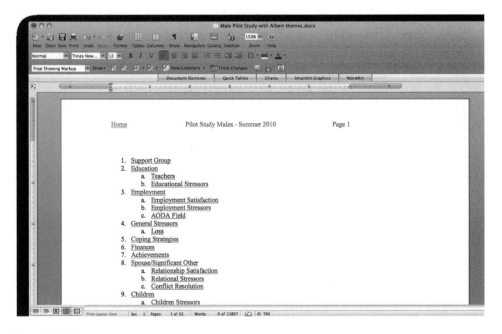

Figure A.1 Themes.

Traditionally, using the constant comparative method, transcriptions would be printed, unitized in pencil, taped onto note cards, and then taped onto an empty wall underneath a heading or major theme. Over time, additional quotes may begin to emerge and increase the data underneath each theme, and many new themes also emerge. A description of how to utilize the constant comparative method in electronic form can be found below. It should be noted that printing the final document and viewing it on a wall is still an option if the researcher values and/or needs a larger visual representation of the data.

A primary strength of electronically organizing qualitative data is that it is then electronically backed up if something were to happen to the data, such as all or a portion of the data being lost or damaged. Additionally, if a qualitative research project becomes physically larger than the space allowed to organize and/or contain the data, then one or multiple Word documents will take care of any space issues, as one merely needs an available computer. It should also be noted that when researchers meet together in a room, it is quite helpful to show the electronic data analysis on the computer screen, but also to show it on a projector screen; many university and college classrooms have these large screens in their classrooms and this does provide for a larger visual of the data.

A limitation of organizing qualitative data electronically is that it loses tangible and visual components compared to organizing research on boards or walls, which many researchers may be accustomed to or prefer. Also, when multiple researchers are tackling the same research project, it can become difficult to organize the electronic data if no one person is designated to compile the unitizations into one document. It is recommended that one person be in charge of organizing and compiling the electronic data; this will help with any confusion or disorganization that may occur among researchers. Also, for some, electronically manipulating data may present challenges if the researchers have difficulty working computers.

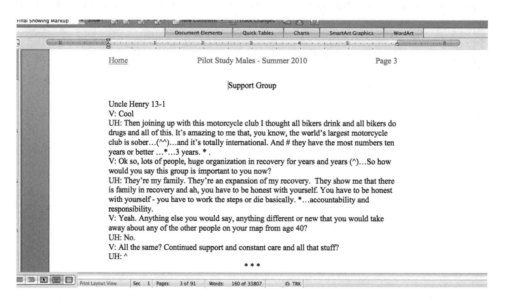

Figure A.2 Transcript sample.

To electronically organize qualitative data, begin with the following:

1 Open a blank Word document.
2 On the first page, create a three-column header by clicking "Header" under the "Insert" toolbar.
  Left: Type "Home"
  Centered: Type the title of the research project
  Right: Insert the page number
3 In the top center of the first page type "Themes."
4 Underneath it, begin an outline of the themes identified during the unitization process.
5 For each heading, retype the headings on the proceeding pages, which is where the unitized segments will be pasted. So if your first theme is "Support Group" then page two should have a centered title called "Support Group" also. All unitized sections that fall under the topic of "Support Group" should be pasted (they were copied from the original transcriptions) under this heading.

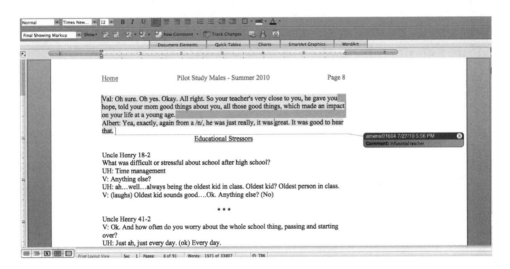

Figure A.3 Pasted units of meaning by theme.

To create a hyperlink that allows easier access to and from your themes, as qualitative data can be lengthy when placed on Word documents, hyperlink your outline to proceeding themes as follows:

1 Highlight the first qualitative theme under your outline.
2 Go to the "Insert" toolbar and click "Bookmark."
3 Title your bookmark with the theme that you are hyperlinking without spaces or punctuation. So "Support Group" would be saved in a bookmark as "SupportGroup."
4 Scroll down to the correlating theme page where unitized data will be placed, and highlight the heading "Support Group."
5 Go to the "Insert" toolbar and click "Hyperlink."

6   The hyperlink will be connected within the document by clicking on bookmarks and then "Support Group."
7   To move from the outline on page one to the correlated unitized theme page, hold down the "Ctrl" key and click on "Support Group."
8   Repeat this step with other themes as needed.
9   The "Home" at the top of the screen on each page can be hyperlinked to the "Outline" word, so that each page you are on can quickly transport you back to your outline to continue with placing the unitized segments under the proper themes.

The above example is one form of electronic data analysis that has been utilized by a research team. There may be other methods to explore and it may be beneficial to explore tweaking this method to suit one's own research needs. Some special considerations include investing in research specific flashdrives or password-protected desktop folders to hold data, as well as monitoring how electronic data is passed on from one researcher to another. As with any computer-based confidential document, emailing electronic data analysis is discouraged to ensure client confidentiality. Additionally, client consent forms and personal identifying information should be kept out of the document.

Closing comment

I have not mentioned any commercial products that are available to aid in conducting qualitative analysis. This is due both to my minimal experience with these products and a reluctance to endorse one product over another.

Appendix B

Introductory comments

The informed consent form that follows was written by students in a senior level class in undergraduate research with the aid of the course instructors. The course was entitled "Qualitative and Interpretative Research Methods Class (PSYC 435)" and was held during the fall term in 2009 at Viterbo University. The members of the class in alphabetical order were: Adam Alexander, Heather Harelstad, Jamie Harris, Shannon Ketcham, Ashley Kirkeng, Val Kokott-Rebhahn, M.A., Richard Morehouse, Ph.D., Sara Moser, and Alyssa Thomas. The project was a mixed methods study of student-athletes who had participated in intercollegiate sports for four years. Each student athlete was interviewed by one of the students or professor in the class. The athletes were also given several paper and pencil instruments to be completed at the time of the interview. Below is the consent form used for this project.

Informed consent form

TITLE OF PROJECT: Understanding the Impact of Sports on Student-Athletes throughout their Lives.

NAME OF INVESTIGATORS: Richard Morehouse (Mort), Ph.D. and Valerie Kokott-Rebhahn (Val), M.A., and students from the Qualitative & Interpretative Research psychology class (PSYC 435).

CONTACT INFORMATION: First instructor contact information
Second instructor contact information
Student researcher contact information

You are invited to participate in a qualitative and interpretative research study on the impact of sports on student-athletes in college. I hope to learn about the positive and negative aspects of being involved in sports throughout a student-athlete's life. I also hope to learn about the role of parents in the lives of student-athletes. You were selected as a possible participant in this study because you are a student-athlete in his/her senior year and/or last year of eligibility to play sports in college, or you are a parent of a student-athlete that meets the just-mentioned requirements.

If you decide to participate, you will be asked to participate in an interview (student-athlete) and complete a few questionnaires (student-athlete and parent). This researcher will take notes during the project. The process should not have much risk involved, but there is the possibility of the topic inducing some stress related to negative memories regarding sports. If you are uncomfortable with talking about a particular topic, we can skip the question if necessary. The benefit you may receive from participating in this study is that you are adding to the body of knowledge on student-athletes, and in particular in regard to parents' information, and you may find that recalling the years in sports activities highlights many positives that you may or may not have thought about.

For the student-athletes, if you give consent to have the interview audio recorded, that will be the procedure with which we will proceed. However, if you are uncomfortable with audio recording, we will not audio record the interview and more rigorous notes will be taken during the interview.

Any information obtained in connection with this study that can be identified with you (both student-athlete and parents) will remain confidential and will be disclosed only with your permission. In any written or oral presentations, no one will be identified or identifiable, unless permission is given. Recordings will be listened to and transcribed by the Qualitative and Interpretative Research class as part of the data analysis process. Discussion will occur in class to also analyze the data.

There will be no compensation given to you for participation in this study.

Your decision whether or not to participate will not affect your future relations with Viterbo University, or the researchers in any way. If you decide to participate, you are free to discontinue participation at any time without affecting such relationships.

If you have any questions, please ask. If you have any additional questions later, I will be happy to answer them. You can reach me, _____, at _____or at _____. My professors, Richard Morehouse (phone number and email address here) and Val Kokott-Rebhahn (phone number and email address here) can also be contacted if necessary with any questions you may have.

You are making a decision whether or not to participate. Your signature indicates that you are 18 years of age, have read the information provided above, and have decided to participate. You may withdraw at any time without prejudice after signing this form should you choose to discontinue participation in this study.

Would you like a signed and dated copy of this form to keep? Yes No

_____   _____

Signature of Participant   Date

_____   _____

Signature of Investigator   Date

Closing comment

The model for the Informed Consent Form was obtained from the Viterbo University Webpage on IRBs (Viterbo University n.d.). The Viterbo University model was used as a skeleton framework for the student to construct the informed consent form. I have found the University's IRB webpage helpful in this and in other research projects.

Appendix C

Introductory comments

The proposal in this appendix was written for a private funding agency and submitted for approval. Therefore this proposal is somewhat different than the proposal outlined in Chapter 7. I selected this proposal even though the agency that it was initially submitted to did not fund it. The project was eventually funded internally and I believe it is helpful to see how the basic elements of a proposal can be modified to meet the requirements of different potential funding agencies. All references to the funding agency that this project was submitted to have been omitted.

The proposal was submitted by an ad hoc research team consisting of four students. I was the faculty sponsor and lead researcher for the project. The names of the students involved are Aleksey Sakharuk, Samantha Merry, Violeta Kadieva, and Mallory Nesberg.

This project proposal is included here as there are other references to it in the body of this book and it illustrates the elements of an inquiry proposal in a somewhat altered form than in outline earlier.

Research proposal

Microgenetic study of the tutoring process: learning center research

Following up on Carol Dweck's (1999, 2006) work on self-theories of intelligence, two students and I have explored the influence of tutors on the students they tutor. We initiated two projects. The first project examined two hypotheses: (1) the effects on tutors' self-theory of intelligence on the self-theories of their students and (2) the second hypothesis examined the influence of tutors' self-theories of intelligence on the test scores in Anatomy and Physiology of their students. This project confirmed both hypotheses and the results were presented at the American Psychological Association annual convention in San Francisco this August (Morehouse et al. 2007). We have also collected data for a second study examining the correlation between self-theories of intelligence (Dweck 1999, 2006) and their approaches to learning (Entwistle 2000). We are in the process of analyzing this data. We anticipate that students who have a growth mindset as measured by Carol Dweck's (1999) self-theory of intelligence scale will have a deep approach to learning as measured by Approaches and Study Skills Inventory for Students [ASSIST] (Tait et al. 1998).

For this project, we are proposing a microgenetic study that explores the process of tutoring. What is the microgenetic method? This method attempts to understand learning and changes in cognitive development by the examination of participants as they engage in the process of learning. Microgenetic studies take place over an extended period of time. Past research using this methodology for analyzing strategies for thinking and problem solving has shown that cognitive changes and learning occurred in a non-linear fashion with strategies moving from more effective to less effective and back to more effective strategies before settling on the most effective strategies (Siegler and Crowley 1991; Kuhn 1995; Siegler 1996).

We are interested in observing the interaction between the students and their tutors as well as the student/student interaction. In our earlier research, we (Morehouse, Sakharuk, and Kadieva 2007) found that tutors with growth mindsets modified the mindsets of the students they tutor. This research also shows that tutors' contribute to the students' development of a more malleable view of intelligence and understanding of effort as it relates to learning. However, the more interesting question to us now is "What is the nature of that relationship?" In other words, what does the process of tutoring look like as it is happening? Noel Entwistle, Bell Professor of Education at the University of Edinburgh writes, "[a] deep strategic approach to studying is generally related to high levels of academic achievement but only where the assessment procedures emphasise and reward personal understanding" (2000, p. 4) while learners with a surface approach tend to do less well.

Entwistle (2000) presents five levels of understanding as outcomes for learning:

- mentioning (incoherent bits of information without any obvious structure),
- describing (brief descriptions of topics derived mainly from material provided),
- relating (outline, personal explanations lacking detail or supporting argument),
- explaining (relevant evidence used to develop structured, independent arguments), and
- conceiving (individual conception of topics developed through reflection) (p. 5).

It is these, among other, levels of understanding that we will be looking at when we review the videotapes of the tutoring sessions. We anticipate seeing these levels of understanding in both tutors and tutees.

Recent research has examined the changes and development in inquiry and argument skills (Kuhn 2005). These skills are closely related to the levels of understanding as presented by Entwistle (2000); Entwistle and Ramsden (1983); Marton and Säljö (1976). Kuhn (2005,1995) has shown that the changes in skills of inquiry and argument change in "fits and starts" – moving two steps forward and one step backwards until a relatively stable level has been secured. Kuhn used an approach to research pioneered by Robert Siegler (Siegler and Crowley 1991) called microgenetic research. This approach looks at change in intense and relatively long duration timeframes. Noel Entwistle has a similar approach to understanding student learning called phenomenography. While Entwistle's approach does not focus on the change process, it shares an orientation to examining learning through detailed microgenetic methods. Based on this work, Entwistle and colleagues (Entwistle and McCune 2004; Marton and Säljö 1976, 1997) have proposed a three-level model for understanding how students approach course content among university students. These approaches are surface, strategic, and deep learning.

As a continuation of our research project in the learning center with students seeking tutoring in Anatomy and Physiology, we are proposing to look closely at two groups of students and their tutors. We will select two groups of students to follow in detail over the course of a semester. One group will be selected based on a tutor with the highest score (most likely a tutor with a growth mindset) on Dweck's Self-theory of Intelligence scale (1999, 2006), and the other group will be selected based on a tutor with the lowest scale score (most likely a tutor with a fixed mindset). We chose the two groups based on the highest and the lowest tutor mindset score in hopes of seeing a clear distinction in approaches to tutoring. We will videotape all the tutoring sessions and transcribe them verbatim. The purpose of the research is to increase understanding of the change process in the skills of inquiry and argument with regard to how students work toward mastering the course material for Anatomy and Physiology. We will also be examining how different styles of tutoring interact with the students' approaches to learning and with their mindsets.

In our recently completed research (Morehouse, Sakharuk, and Kadieva 2007), we found that tutors who have a mindset that sees intelligence as something that can be improved by hard work have a positive influence on the grades of their students. All tutors also contributed to the development of a mindset closer to the mindsets of their tutors.

We anticipate that this research will continue to aid in understanding some of the approaches to teaching-learning of tutors as well as their perspective on the nature of intelligence, and the role of the skills of inquiry and argument on the students they tutor. What we would like to examine is a more fine-grained picture of what the tutoring is like session by session. In order to discover some of the details of the tutoring process we are proposing to videotape the tutoring sessions during the semester.

Method

All the tutors and their students who are seeking tutoring will be given the Entwistle ASSIST instrument (2006) and Dweck's self-theories of intelligence scale (1999) in a pre- and post-test. Two tutoring groups will be videotaped based on the score on tutors' on the self-theories of intelligence scale (Dweck 1999). Beginning about the third week of classes the two tutor/student group sessions will be videotaped. After each videotaped session, the tapes will be transcribed verbatim. A microgenetic analysis of the transcripts will be conducted – to be completed by 15th July 2008.

This mixed method approach will examine both the changes in students' and tutors' scores on ASSIST and self-theories of intelligence scale (1999) as well as a microgenetic assessment of each transcript.

Data analysis

Two types of analysis will be completed. First, there will be a straightforward correlation of the ASSIST scores (Tait, Entwistle, and McCune 1998) and the self-theories of intelligences (Dweck 1999) scores as well as pre-post comparisons.

The next type of analysis will be the microgenetic phase. This phase will include the reading and rereading of the transcripts for all the videotapes. Then the transcripts are broken into units of meaning (Maykut and Morehouse 1994). These units of meaning will be organized using the constant comparison method. The microgenetic analysis of the videotaped tutoring sessions will provide a picture of change and continuity within the tutoring process.

Final results will integrate the statistical findings and the microgenetic (qualitative) findings. This will include individual student profiles as well as a profile of the process of tutoring session by session and a pre and post comparison on the two scales used in the study (Tait, Entwistle and McCune 1998; Dweck 1999).

Concluding statement

In Robert Siegler's seminal work, *Emerging Minds: The process of change in children's thinking*, he argues that we reformulate our basic assumptions regarding children's thinking by looking anew at the kinds of questions we ask, "the mechanisms we propose to explain it and the basic metaphors that underlie our thinking about it" (1996, p. 218). Carol Dweck's work as presently articulated allows for movement from one mindset to another, the question that a microgenetic analysis might contribute to understanding is how this movement occurs. Likewise, Entwistle's work on approaches to learning allows for change but does not provide an understanding of what elements contribute to students making those changes or their nonlinear nature. Our study is designed to provide deeper knowledge of this change process.

Appendix D

Introductory comments

The following is an evaluation project also conducted with a group of students. The project was an evaluation of a summer residential experience in which high school students attended courses designed specifically to illustrate the accessibility of a post-secondary education to students not normally bound for college. The design of the courses was oriented to challenge the students on material that was intrinsically interesting to them. One course was called Sustainability and focused on understanding and addressing environmental issues within the local community. The other course was Forensics and was modeled after crime-solving by using forensic evidence grounded in biology and chemistry to solve a made-up crime.

I did the initial group interviews and the students, along with my co-instructor, Valerie Kokott-Rebhahn, conducted the data analysis. The data analysis was a part of a training exercise to acquaint students with the ways of qualitative analysis before they undertook their own project. Students transcribed the group interviews and conducted the data analysis using the constant comparative method. This training exercise had the added advantage of getting the student excited about the research process.

Here is the final report from this project.

DPI (Summer Scholars Program) Evaluation

(Richard E Morehouse, Valerie Kokott-Rebhahn, Adam Alexander, Heather Harelstad, Jamie Harris, Shannon Ketcham, Ashley Kirkeng, Sarah Moser, and Alyssa Thomas)

The stated purpose of the Summer Scholars Program is to "encourage and prepare students to attend college after high school" (dpi.wi.gov/weop/precol.html). In order to become university students, the potential students need to first see themselves as somewhat like other university students, see themselves as able to start a college education, and also able to meet the challenges of college work (Bandura 1997). Self-efficacy is the internal mechanism that regulates one's ability to produce a desired or intended result. "Unless people believe they can produce desired results and forestall detrimental ones by their actions, they have little incentive to act or preserve in the face of difficulty" (Bandura 2001: 19).

As our group interview data indicated many students do not think that college was for "kids like us" when they enrolled in the program. So the question is: If students don't see themselves as potential college students, how can that perspective be changed? An answer may be found in Albert Bandura's work on agency (2001) and self-efficacy (1997). In a study specifically looking at self-efficacy and academic continuance and achievement, Bandura and colleagues found that "students' perceived efficacy in regulation of their learning activities at a junior high school level contributed to their academic achievement in high school and their likelihood of completing their high school education" (Caprara *et al.* 2008: 532). He argues that a person will work toward a goal, and persist in the pursuit of that goal if they have a sense of self-efficacy (Bandura 1997). The Summer Scholars Program at Viterbo University was set up with Bandura's self-efficacy in mind. By giving students both something that is interesting and challenging, and an opportunity to achieve success with others perceived to be like themselves, a potential for change is opened up to these students. Accordingly, two programs were made available to the students: Forensics (solving a criminal case study using chemistry and biology as tools) and Sustainability (using a case study model to understand ecological problems using the tools of business and ecology). Additionally, students were provided information about the nature of college, college application process, and study skills. The program eased participants into thinking about themselves as potential college students.

Self-efficacy provided a framework for program development as well as a lens through which to evaluate the program. Students' comments on their involvement in the Summer Scholars Program indicate that there were changes in their attitudes that are consistent with a positive sense of self-efficacy regarding their likelihood of attending college and a growing sense of personal agency. The Summer Scholars faculty also noticed changes in these student attitudes. This developing sense of self-efficacy and agency are connected with several of the other findings of the program, i.e. student enjoyment of the college experience, their statements about program and their involvement in a "mini-college" experience, the way they saw themselves as learners, their changing perspective on the nature of college, the way they think about the future and their potential careers.

Methods

Among the mechanisms of personal agency, none is more central or pervasive than people's beliefs in their capacity to exercise some measure of control over their functioning and over events (Bandura 1997). Efficacy beliefs are the foundation of human agency. A variety of instruments was used to assess changes in student attitude during the Summer Scholars program. All the instruments selected or developed are intended to gain some sense of student's self-efficacy.

Students attending the Summer Scholars Program held at Viterbo University during the summer of 2009 participated in one of two academic courses (Forensics or Sustainability) as well as jointly receiving instruction about the nature of college, its admissions processes, and a variety of study skills. The evaluation of the program was in five parts. First students were given a pre- and post-test using three instruments: *ASSIST* (used in Instrument 1) that provides a view of the way of students approached their role in getting a handle on course content. Carol Dweck's *Self-theory of Intelligence* (1999, used in Instrument 2) examines the influence of a malleable view of intelligence (called a Growth Mindset) compared to a static view of intelligence (called a Fixed Mind Set). Both of these instruments are widely used in research directed toward understanding students' attitudes (Dweck 1999 and others; Entwistle 2000 and others). An additional instrument was developed for this study called the Self-Management Inventory (Morehouse 2009 – see Instrument 3). The instructor in the Forensics and Sustainability program as well as the instructor in the skills program completed an evaluation matrix (see Observation Matrix). Finally, at the end of the week, students participated in a group interview regarding their assessment of the program. A fifth on-line assessment was planned but was not executed. We had planned to conduct an on-line follow-up of students in the program but we were unable to access all the students by email and those few we did contact did not respond. We will attempt to contact these students during the spring semester.

Result

The results of the assessment were mixed. There were strong gains in the instructor's Observational Matrix and positive support for the program from the student group interviews. The pre-post instruments showed a positive direction but the sample was too small to show any statistical change.

Pre/Post assessment of attitudes toward study

Three separate self-report instruments were used to measure changes in student attitudes that have been closely connected to student success in academic programs. Two of the instruments (ASSIST and Self-Theories of Intelligences – adult scale) have been widely used and extensively evaluated for their validity and reliability (Entwistle 2005; Dweck 1999). The other instrument (Cognitive-Assessment and Interpersonal Inventory) was developed specifically for this study (Morehouse 2009).

Over a period of 30 years a group of scholars headed by Noel Entwistle developed a series of instruments measuring whether students approached learning from a deep perspective, that is, the saw knowledge as being applied to their lives, connected to other knowledge they possessed and approachable by using intellectual or academic skills. Other students approach learning from a surface perspective, seeing knowledge as fragmented pieces to be memorized and later discarded. One way to track progress is by the way they move from mentioning things (surface), to describing events (surface), to relating personal ways of expressing ideas but without supporting evidence (beginning deep), to explaining ideas using relevant evidence (deep), and to reflecting on the meaning and application of concepts (deep). ASSIST measures students' attitudes toward these approaches to study using a series of questions (25 on the short form).

The ASSIST scores of the students in the Summer Scholars Program move in the direction of increased deep approaches (place average scores here) to study and away from surface approaches study (place average scores here). No statistical analysis was done beyond the use of mean scores because the sample was too small for meaningful statistical analysis. However, it is worth noting that the mean scores all moved in a positive and predicted direction.

Carol Dweck has an extensive body of work examining the relationship between how students and others view the malleability of intelligence in themselves and others (Dweck 1999, 2006). She and her colleagues developed an instrument widely used to explore how self-theories of intelligence influence students' academic efforts especially in the face of challenge and adversity. Students with a malleable view of their own intelligence (I can get smarter if I work hard) are more likely to persist in a project even when the project is beyond their ability to solve the problem, whereas students with a fixed theory of intelligence (My intelligence will remain the same no matter what I do) are likely to give up more quickly on these challenging tasks. The students with a malleable sense of intelligence Dweck calls incremental theorists (or having a Growth Mindset), while students who see intelligence as unchangeable she calls entity theorists (or having a Fixed Mindset).

As with the ASSIST measures, the students' scores on the self-theory of intelligence were too small to do a statistical analysis. Again, we did compute mean averages for the students' deep and surface scores. The mean score moved in a positive (from Fixed Mindset toward Growth Mindset) and predicted direction.

Cognitive self-assessment and interpersonal inventory

The cognitive self-assessment and interpersonal inventory (Morehouse 2009) was developed to more closely measure the specific objectives of the Summer Scholars Program. Small, non-statistical changes occurred on the self-assessment and interpersonal inventory.

The three-assessment instruments all tended in the same direction and supported the students' assessment of the program from the group interviews and the Observational Matrix finding compiled by the course instructors. Again, the gains were small and non-statistical due in part to the small sample size.

Assessment of group using an observation matrix (average of both groups)

The Assessment of Groups using the Observational Matrix (OM) was developed for assessing group participation in Biology Lab (Early and Morehouse 2008). It assesses work habits, teamwork, and instructor expectation. It also addresses the basic skills of listening, speaking, and reasoning. It has not been subjected to rigorous reliability or validity study, but has been used by a number of Viterbo instructors as one method for tracking student engagement over time (Early 1999) and found to be helpful for instructional purposes. The results of the pre-post assessment of student participation in the lab sessions for Forensics and Sustainability classes and the skills classes attended by both groups is presented in Table A.1.

Table A.1 Results of the pre-post assessment of student participation.

Questions	Observation at beginning	Observation at end	Difference
Asks clear and direct questions of partners	1.8	3.3	1.5 +
Register agreement/ disagreement with partner	2.3	3.3	1 +
Restate problems or summarize ideas	1.5	3	1.5 +
Seeks clarification from partner when needed	2.3	3.5	1.2 +
When stuck, first ask partner then instructor	2.5	3.5	1 +
Speaks to partner in an engaging and friendly manner	3.3	3.6	1.3 +
Shows interest in partner's ideas	3	4	1 +
Deals well with criticism from partner	1.8	3	1.2 +
Encourages partner to join conversation	2.3	3	.7 +
Displays curiosity	2	3.6	1.6 +
Respects partner's ideas	2.6	4	1.4 +
Respects partner when he/she is being directed by partner	1.8	3.3	1.5 +
Does not monopolize discussion with partner	1.8	3.6	1.8 +

No attempt was made to conduct a statistical analysis of this data, as the sample is too small to gain statistically significant results. It is clear from the positive changes in the instructor ratings that the instructors saw a positive change in attitudes and behaviors among the students in their classes. These assessments were based on daily observations plus the final project presented by students in both content classes (Forensics and Sustainability).

Qualitative analysis of group interviews

It is partly based on efficacy beliefs that people choose what challenges to undertake, how much effort to expend in the endeavor, how long to persevere in the face of obstacles and failure, and whether failures are motivational or demoralizing. The likelihood that people will act on the outcomes they expect prospective performance to produce depends on their beliefs about whether or not they can produce those performances. A strong sense of coping efficacy reduces vulnerability to stress and depression in the taxing situation and strengthens resiliency to adversity (Bandura 2001: 19).

The goals of the Summer Scholars Program includes introducing students to understanding the college application process, how to complete financial aid, the nature of residential life, student services, and the number of people who complete a college education. If students both know what they need to do and develop the self-efficacy to complete an undergraduate education, they are more likely to apply to a university.

All students participated in a group interview organized by course content (Forensics or Sustainability). A semi-structured interview schedule was prepared for the interviews. The evaluator, who did not participate in any of the instructional or extracurricular activities, conducted the interviews. The interviews lasted about 45 minutes and were audio-recorded. The recordings were transcribed verbatim. A research team of seven students and two instructors analyzed the data using the constant comparative method (Maykut and Morehouse 1994). The findings from the group interviews are presented below.

A growing sense of self-efficacy and skill development

Self-efficacy and skill acquisition go hand-in-hand. Students in the interview talked about the content and skills they were learning as well as what they thought they would do in the near future with that knowledge and those skills. Bandura writes that people choose "what challenges to undertake, how much effort to expend in the endeavor, how long to persevere in the face of obstacles and failure..." (2001: 19) based partly on their efficacy beliefs. Students appear to have developed a sense of self-efficacy regarding their ability to get into and complete a college education.

One student in the Forensics class illustrates that learning how to do a task leads to enthusiasm and potentially to further study. He stated:

* *Yea, well, when we were doing the fingerprints and stuff, I was so hyped up and psyched for it, it was just to (using false excited voice) ah there's fingerprints, oh we can ...*
* *Rest (Laughing)*
* *I was just getting really excited for it. So it made me more interested in the, kind of like the, criminal justice type stuff.*

Other students in the Sustainability class talked about how seeing others work on environmental issues helped them to think about what they might do themselves. The student said:

* *What stuck out for me was um ... how the teachers talked about the "restore" which I think was really cool that La Crosse is actually doing something to help like the community and that makes me want to be involved in our community stuff in ... back in our town.*

Efficacy beliefs also play a key role in shaping the directions lives take by influencing the types of activities and environments people choose to get into. Any factor that influences choice of behavior can profoundly affect the direction of personal development. This is because the social influences operating in selected environments continue to promote certain competencies, values, and interests long after the decisional determinant has rendered its inaugurating effects. Thus, by choosing and shaping their environment, people can have a hand in what they become (Bandura 2001: 10–11). The likelihood that people will act on a particular project depends on what they expect their actions will produce. If they have had some success with a similar project, they are more likely to engage in a new project. This attitude (self-efficacy) strengthens with each success. A strong sense of coping efficacy reduces vulnerability to stress and depression in the taxing situation and strengthens resiliency to adversity (Bandura 2001: 19). One student talked about seeing his efforts at working with the fingerprinting equipment in a way that illustrated a growing confidence.

- *Um it was pretty sweet to see all the finger prints, off of stuff like in /a/ or a pop can and uh, just pretty much analyze all the information that we are given, just to find some, uh, real facts that we could put into our slide show and stuff.*

People can also increase a person's sense of efficacy by showing what is possible. One student commented about an inspirational speaker who presented on campus.

- *Yesterday we had, uh, um, some talks from some people and the one that really stuck out was the dancer that, um, Nancy that talked about her story of life was really cool and inspiring.*

Another student was more general when talking about inspirational people. She stated:

- *I'd probably talk to, ah talk to, actually meet the people for motivation that inspires people, cause; I met a lot of people that inspired me ...*

The atmosphere created by the Summer Scholars Program appears to have had a positive impact on the attitudes of the participants regarding attending college. These attitudes are also seen in the other sections of the group interviews as they were in the Observational Matrix.

Students' positive and negative statements about the program

Most of the student comments were positive. The newness of the location and campus life were highlights for the participants. Here are a couple of comments about being on campus and in a new city.

- *It's fun... it's a new experience. You'll probably do something that you would never do, or if you came here.*
- *La Crosse is a nice place, it's ... I, I like experiencing not only the college but the area around it ... and it's was cool getting to see how the people are like and I think downtown is really great. It's very nice and ... I don't know it kind go give you a sense of new areas and sometimes it put into consideration of actually moving somewhere different for college ... and experiencing a whole new area, not just a new college but a whole new city maybe!*
- *I like how we pretty much got to live the college life for a little while and kind of see what it's like to live in the dorms ... with a roommate ... that you hate [Everyone laughs].*

While these comments may seem somewhat superficial, experiencing a city and a campus from the inside-out creates the possibility that the students might see themselves actually attending a college sometime in the near future.

One student made a "being there" comment about participating in the forensic lab.

• *The labs and how, you really don't think that it's that complicated with trying to find our ... like on TV or just that ... they make it look so simple and then you get behind the scenes and everything is so much more complicated than what it seems.*

Looking at the group interviews as a whole, students strongly valued the experience of "being in college" rather than just visiting a college. They, even within the four days they were on campus, thought of their experience as a college experience. The dorm life, the university level of instruction, the forays into the city all contributed to this college experience.

Participants saw themselves as learning

Most students talked about the skills that they had learned during the program. A number of the students talked about what might be called "process skills." These are skills necessary to work in groups and solve complex problems. These are some of their comments.

• *I, I learned how to work better in a group to contribute, and how to like, to share everyone's ideas, not just ...talking.*
• *Um, I think the Sustainability class has taught me to be more aware of like my surroundings and like how my actions could impact the world.*

Other students learned what they didn't know or what they needed to improve on as students. These insights are stated below.

• *Well, I would like to work on like studying more, the correct way since I don't really know how to study right.*
• *We really need to use [free time] for study.*

At least two students stated that what they learned should be brought back to their home communities and school.

• *Um, I think the Sustainability class has taught me to be more aware of like my surroundings and like how my actions could impact the world.*
• *You have to tell like I want to tell them [the kids back home], "you're doing, you're not even doing the right thing, and first of all you're not even paying attention.*

What they learned that had relevance to their future plans. One student commented on the importance of the information for their daily lives.

• *But, it's [the Sustainability classes] good information to just understand. It's like it's good basic information that we can all use ... like it doesn't necessarily need to be used in our careers, but it can just be used in our daily lives.*

Other students commented about inspiration generated by the program.

- *Um, well, just coming to this program it gave me a lot of inspiration to keep on trying, you know, go further in my life and do my goals.*
- *Well I'm going to say, um, the teacher there that we had for the Sustainability session, um, I think made me realize that there are a lot of people that really care about the environment and everything …*

Still other students looked to the specific courses for what was important to them during the Summer Scholars Program.

- *There's so many different parts to it [forensics], there's a lot of careers that have to really come together just to solve one case …*
- *Uh, well what I would like to say was just the same thing that Dona said, um about sustainability, just the class itself, kind of, because like, um, of course I took that class and like it taught me some stuff that I didn't like really know about the environment and so / ? /. It was an eye opening [class].*
- *It taught me "How to go green."*

Finally, one student's comment about learning cannot be ignored. The student said, "You meet a lot of crazy people," which was met by supportive laughter from the whole group. This comment speaks to the ways students learned to get along with new people and to the expectations and fears that they brought to the program. The "crazy people" the student was talking about were now their assembled friends.

- *It kind of makes me want to go to a school more like this, since it's more private and smaller, and I don't want to be stuck in like a lecture hall with 300 other kids, where, you're not probably going to get as much help as you would here.*

One student commented about a skill she was learning.

- *I, I learned how to work better in a group to contribute, and how to like, to share everyone's ideas, not just … talking.*

Here are three different ways that the Summer Scholar Program contributed to students' efficacy regarding college. The first comment is about the general impact of the program, the second about applying science in a fun way, and the third is on the influence of an inspirational speaker. Each statement supports a sense of efficacy regarding college achievement.

- *Um, well, just coming to this program it gave me a lot of inspiration to keep on trying, you know, go further in my life and do my goals.*
- *Um it was pretty sweet to see all the finger prints, off of stuff like in /a/ or a pop can and uh, just pretty much analyze all the information that we are given, just to find some, uh, real facts that we could put into our slide show and stuff.*
- *Yesterday we had uh um same talks from some people and the one that really stuck out was the dancer that, um, Nancy that talked about her story of life was really cool and inspiring.*

Enjoying the college experience

In addition to finding inspiration in the program, students also enjoyed their experience. While enjoyment is not always a criteria for determining the effectiveness of the program, a case can be made that enjoyment is important to attitude changes. If students do not perceive that college will be enjoyable, they are not likely to attend, much less persist.

One student commented:

- *It's fun... it's a new experience. You'll probably do something that you would never do, or if you came here.*

Another student commented about the value of living like college students – getting a real college experience.

- *I like how we pretty much got to live the college life for a little while and kind of see what it's like to live in the dorms ... with a roommate ... that you hate [Everyone laughs].*

The value of a real college experience extended to the classes as well.

- *The labs and how, you really don't think that it's that complicated with trying to find our ... like on TV or just that ... they make it look so simple and then you get behind the scenes and everything is so much more complicated that what it seems.*

The location also played a part in making the experience enjoyable. While La Crosse may have some unique attributes which contribute to a positive orientation of the students, it is more likely that the experience of moving to a small campus in a medium-size city contributed to these positive attitudes. A student commented about being in the city as follows:

- *La Crosse is a nice place, it's ... I, I like experiencing not only the college but the area around it ... and it's was cool getting to see how the people are like and I think downtown is really great. It's very nice and ... I don't know it kind go give you a sense of new areas and sometimes it put into consideration of actually moving somewhere different for college ... and experiencing a whole new area, not just a new college but a whole new city maybe!*

Students' overall impressions of the experience

The students reported that they were learning and that they were enjoying the learning experiences, even though it was often challenging. A wide variety of people and experiences contributed to their appreciation of the "college experience." The first comment is about the intrinsic value of what the students in the sustainability class were learning.

- *But, it's [the Sustainability classes] good information to just understand. It's like it's good basic information that we can all use ... like it doesn't necessarily need to be used in our careers, but it can just be used in our daily lives.*

The next several comments are about the way individual people affected student enjoyment and appreciation of the program.

- *I'd probably talk to, ah talk to, actually meet the people for motivation that inspires people, cause; I met a lot of people that inspired me*
- *Well I'm going to say, um, the teacher there that we had for the sustainability session, um, I think made me realize that there are a lot of people that really care about the environment and everything*

Beliefs (past and present) about college

Even though these participants had not been to college and did not know many people in their immediate circle of friends and family who had, they came to the program with ideas about the nature of the college experience. The combination of "living" the college experience, even for a short time, plus being provided with specific information about Viterbo University and its policies and procedures, appears to have changed many of the participants' perspectives on college life. Here are the comments of several students about their changing ideas about college.

- *It turns out it's a lot more fun.*
- *Uh, well I always thought that college was for really smart kids. Like the really good students in the class but like they accept like students with GPAs of like 2.5.*
- *Well I kinda thought that college wasn't possible for like certain people but then actually college is actually possible for everyone it just depends of you want to go to college or not.*

The last two statements are particularly important as they relate to one of the stated goals of the program – to encourage and prepare students to attend college after high school.

Other students talked about becoming aware that they might fit into college life – something that was not in their outlook earlier. These comments varied from awareness of the variety of things available in college to seeing themselves like young people who are attending college. Several students commented:

- *You can just do intramural [sports] for fun.*
- *I learned you can go to college undecided.*
- *It's not just studying here, it's just becoming part of a college and meeting other, different people.*

These students commented on what changed about their perspective of college and their possibility for attending college.

- *I usually thought college was for very smart people, but since I've come here and learned more about it, I learned that I, uh, I also have a chance.*
- *I thought it would be kind of – more complicated ... but really, when they break it down, they gave us each like orientation and then finding a career after, and they actually really give you a lot more [re]sources than I thought.*

Students also talked about the affordability of college, both private and public colleges.

These changes in what college is like have a potential to influence future decisions to attend college. These students are more likely, at least, to apply to college after a positive experience with a college-like experience (Bandura 1997).

Talk about potential careers

The program seems to have stimulated some of the students to begin thinking about careers. Here are some of their comments.

- *I started thinking about where I would go from here.*
- *Cause I want to be a green architect and build houses that are … and green and sustainable.*
- *I've always wanted to be a teacher, so after hearing Lisa, talk about how her school and the teachers over there helping children, it makes me feel like, it's possible if I want to help kids – cause that's what I want to do.*
- *It is a good place to start [DPI summer scholars program] to like learn how to do [college admissions] and probably a good thing to put on a résumé.*
- *There's so many different parts to it [forensics], there's a lot of careers that have to really come together just to solve one case.*
- *It [forensics] may be something I could really get into. I thought it was kinda fun, ah, seems like it's be pretty easy … you just got to be patient.*
- *Some of it was a kind of new backup plan, like if I decide not to do what I want to do; I can have a backup plan.*
- *I want to do more research on it [career options in chemistry and biology] before I like get myself into it.*

These students not only began to think about careers but began to see themselves as potentially pursuing those careers.

Future programs

Students had some ideas about how to improve the program. Somewhat surprisingly, students commented on the need for more work about other suggestions. Here are their comments regarding future Summer Scholars Programs.

- *Maybe we could actually, like actually be active and do something with, within the city and like go to a park and plant trees and clean up things.*
- *Well, I would like to work on like studying more, the correct way since I don't really know how to study right.*
- *We really need to use [free time] for study.*

These comments also indicate that they took the program seriously. As other comments indicate, they also enjoyed themselves.

Summary

The program seems to have accomplished its major goal. While the pre-post tests were inconclusive, the Observational Matrix, and the student comments in the group interview all indicate that the program was well conceived and executed. This report ends with one final quote from a student talking about the Sustainability course. In responding to what they would take home with them from the program, she said:

- *You have to tell, like I want to tell them (the kids back home), "you're doing, you're not even doing the right thing, and first of all you're not even paying attention."*

Instruments

Instrument 1

See Dweck, C. (1999). Self-theories: Their role in motivation, personality, and development, New York: Psychology Press.
The instrument was modified using *Key Life Skills: Cognitive, self-management, and interpersonal*, retrieved from www.csulb.edu/~tstevens/h54confi.htm#life skills and life success.

Instrument 2

ASSIST: See Centre for Research on Learning and Instruction (2006) *Approaches and Study Skills Inventory for Students (ASSIST)*, Edinburgh: University of Edinburgh Press.

Instrument 3

Observation matrix[1]

Criteria for evaluation	Strong Demonstrates the ability more than once and does so effectively and naturally.	Developing Demonstrates the ability at least once but not very effectively and it appears forced.	Emerging Attempt is made to demonstrate ability but ineffectively.	Unsatisfactory No attempt is made to demonstrate these characteristics.
Student asks clear and direct questions of partners.				
Student registers agreement or disagreement with partners.				
Student restates problems or summarizes ideas.				
Student seeks clarification from partners when needed.				
Student asks partners questions first and then goes to the instructor only after the group is stuck.				
Student speaks to partners in a manner that is welcoming rather than hostile or combative.				
Student appears interested in partners' ideas.				
Student deals well with criticism from partners.				
Student encourages partners to join in conversation.				
Student displays curiosity about the subject.				
Student respects partners' ideas.				
Student respects lab partners when they attempt to direct the lab session.				
Student does not monopolize discussion within lab partner group.				
Student offers constructive criticism to lab partners in a considerate way.				
Student avoids jumping to conclusions and respects the lab process.				

NOTE

[1] Matrix adapted from the introduction to David Kennedy, *Thinking Trees and Laughing Cats*, (New Jersey: Institute for the Advancement of Philosophy for Children, 2003) by Sheila Early and Richard Morehouse, 2008.

Closing comments

This evaluation project provides some sense of how I attempted to assess student appreciation for the learning experience using qualitative and quantitative data. While the number of students in the classes was small, all the students participated in the group interview and completed all of the assessment instruments. More robust findings may have occurred if a larger group of students had been involved in the project.

Bibliography

American Educational Research Association (2006) Standards for reporting on empirical social science research in AERA publications, *Educational Researcher*, 35(6): 33–40.

American Educational Research Association (2009) Standards for reporting on humanities-oriented research in AERA publications, *Educational Researcher*, 38(6): 481–486.

American Psychological Association (2009a) *Publication Manual of the American Psychological Association*, sixth edition Washington, DC: American Psychological Association.

American Psychological Association (2009b) *Concise Rules of the American Psychological Association (APA) Style*, Washington, DC: American Psychological Association.

Antaki, C. and Widdicombe, S. (eds.) (1998) *Identities in Talk*, London: Sage.

Apple, M. W., Au, W., and Gandin, L. A. (eds.) (2009) *The Routledge International Handbook of Critical Education*, London: Routledge.

Apple, M. W., Ball, S. J., and Gandin, L. A. (eds.) (2011) *The Routledge International Handbook of the Sociology of Education*, London: Routledge.

Argyris, A., Spyrou, T., and Darzentas, J. (2010) Toward the naturalization of agency based on an interactive account of autonomy, *New Ideas in Psychology*, 28(3): 296–311.

Bandura, A. (2001) Social cognitive theory: an agentic perspective, *Annual Review of Psychology*, 52: 1–26.

Bandura, A. (1997) *Self-efficacy: The exercise of control*, New York: Freeman

Banks, J. A. (ed.) (2009) *The Routledge International Companion to Multicultural Education*, London: Routledge

Barrett, T. (2010) The problem-based learning process as finding and being in flow, *Innovations in Education and Teaching International*, 47(2): 165–174.

Belenky, M. F., Clinch, B. M., Goldberger, N. R., and Tarule, J. M. (1986) *Women's Ways of Knowing: The development of self, voice, and mind*, New York: Basic Books.

Bickhard, M. H. (2009) Interactivism: A manifesto, *New Ideas in Psychology*, 27(1): 85–95.

Bishop R. C. (2007) *The Philosophy of the Social Sciences*, London: Continuum.

Boisvert, R. (1998) *John Dewey: rethinking our time*, Albany: NY: SUNY Press.

BrainyQuote (n.d.) www.brainyquote.com/quotes/quotes/a/alberteins162052.html (retrieved March 9, 2011).

Bredo, E. (2009) Comments on Howe: Getting over the methodology wars, *Educational Researcher*, 38(6): 441–448.

Brentano, F. (1995) *Psychology from an Empirical Standpoint*, ed. Linda L. McAlister, London: Routledge.

Brinkmann, S. (2009) Facts, values, and the naturalistic fallacy in psychology, *New Ideas in Psychology*, 27(1): 1–17.

Brown, A. L. (1997) Transforming schools into communities of thinking and learning about serious matters, *American Psychologist*, 52(4): 399–413.

Bruner, J. S. (1990) *Acts of Meaning*, Cambridge, MA: Harvard University Press.

Bruner, J. S. (1996) *The Culture of Education*, Cambridge, MA: Harvard University Press.

Camic, P. M., Rhodes, J. E., and Yardley, L. (2003) Naming the stars: integrating qualitative methods into psychological research, in P. M. Camic, J. E. Rhodes, and L. Yardley (eds.), *Qualitative Research in Psychology: Expanding perspectives in methodology and design*, Washington, DC: American Psychological Association.

Caprara, G., Fida, R., Vecchione, M., Del Bove, G. M., Vecchio, C., Barbaranelli, C., and Bandura, A. (2008). Longitudinal analysis of the role of perceived self-efficacy for self-regulated learning in academic continuance and achievement, *Journal of Educational Psychology*, 100(3): 525– 534.

Centre for Research on Learning and Instruction (2006) *Approaches and Study Skills Inventory for Students (ASSIST)*, Edinburgh: University of Edinburgh.

Cole, M., Engestrom, Y., and Vasquez, O. (eds.) (1997) *Mind, Culture, and Activity: Seminal papers from the laboratory of comparative human cognition*, Cambridge: Cambridge University Press.

Creswell, J. W. (2009) *Research Design: Qualitative, quantitative, and mixed methods approaches*, Thousand Oaks, CA: Sage

Damon, W. (1998) *Handbook of Child Development Vol. 1: Theoretical models of development*, R. M. Lerner (vol. ed.), fifth edition, New York: John Wiley and Sons.

Damon, W. (1998) *Handbook of Child Development Vol. 2: Cognition, perception, and language*, D. Kuhn, R. S. Siegler, and R. M. Lerner (vol. eds.), fifth edition, New York: John Wiley and Sons.

Damon, W. (1998) *Handbook of Child Development Vol. 3: Social, emotional, and personality development*, N. Einsenberg, (vol. ed.), fifth edition, New York: John Wiley and Sons.

Damon, W. (1998) *Handbook of Child Development Vol. 4: Child psychology in practice*, I. E. Sigel and K. A. Renningger, (vol. eds.), fifth edition, New York: John Wiley and Sons.

Damon, W. and Lerner, R. (eds.) (2006) *Handbook of Child Psychology*, sixth edition, New York: John Wiley and Sons.

Davidson, D. (1994) Psychology as philosophy, in M. Martin and L. C. McIntyre (eds.) *Readings in the Philosophy of Social Science*, Cambridge, MA: MIT Press, pp. 79–89.

Davies, B. and Harré, R. (1999) Positioning and personhood, in R. Harré and L. Van Langenhove (eds.), *Positioning Theory: Moral Contexts of Intentional Action*, Malden, MA: Blackwell, pp. 32–52.

Day, C., Sammons, P. and Gu, Q. (2008) Combining qualitative and quantitative methodologies in research on teachers' lives, work, and effectiveness from integration to synergy, *Educational Researcher*, 37(6): 330–342.

Denzin, N. K. and Lincoln, Y. S. (eds.) (2000) *Handbook of Qualitative Research*, second edition, Thousand Oaks, CA: Sage.

Dewey, J. (1922) *Human Nature and Conduct: An introduction to social psychology*, New York: The Modern Library.

Dewey, J (1988) *The Later Works, 1925–1953, Volume 4: The quest for certainty: a study of the relationship of knowledge and action*, Carbondale, IL: Southern Illinois University Press.

Dilthey, W. (1988 [1923]) *Introduction to the Human Sciences: An attempt to lay a foundation for the study of society and history*, trans. R. J. Betanzos, Detroit, MI: Wayne State University Press.

Dweck, C. S. (1999) *Self-theories: Their role in motivation, personality, and development*, London: Psychological Press.

Dweck, C. S. (2006) Mindset: *The new psychology of success*, New York: Random House.

Early, S. M. (2008) *Friendship in Lab Situations: Student and lab instructor perspectives*, La Crosse, WI: Viterbo University unpublished undergraduate paper.

Elliot, A. J. and Dweck, C. S. (eds.) (2005) *Handbook of Competence and Motivation*, New York: Guilford Press.

Entwistle, N. J. (2000) *Promoting Deep Learning through Teaching and Assessment: Conceptual frameworks and educational contexts*, paper presented at the TLRP Conference, Leicester, November 2000 online, available at: www.tlrp.org/acadpub/Entwistle2000.pdf (retrieved March 9, 2011).

Entwistle, N. J. (2006) *ASSIST Approaches and Study Skills Inventory for Students* (short version), Edinburgh: Centre for Research on Learning and Instruction University of Edinburgh.

Entwistle, N. J. and McCune, V. S. (2005) The conceptual bases of study strategy inventories, *Educational Psychology Review*, 16(4): 325–346.

Entwistle, N. J. and Ramsden, P. (1983) *Understanding Student Learning*, London: Croom Helm.

Entwistle N. J., Tait, H., and McCune, V. (2000) Patterns of response to an approach to studying inventory across contrasting groups and contexts, *European Journal of the Psychology of Education*, 15(1): 33–48.

Fine, M. and Torre, M. A. (2004) Re-membering exclusion: Participatory action research in public institutions, *Qualitative Research in Psychology*, 1(1): 12–37.

Firestone, W. A. (1990) Accommodation: Toward a paradigm-praxis dialogue, in E. G. Guba (ed.) *The Paradigm Dialogue*, Beverly Hills, CA: Sage, pp. 105–124.

Fischer, K. W. and Bidell, T. R. (1998) Dynamic development of psychological structures in action and thought, in W. Damon (ed.), *Handbook of Child Development Vol. 1: Theoretical models of human development*, fifth edition, New York: Wiley, pp. 467–561.

Flanagan, O. (1984) *The Science of the Mind*, Cambridge, MA: Bradford Books, The MIT Press.

Gadamer, H. G. (1975) *Truth and Method*, trans. and ed. J. Weinsheimer and D. G. Marshall, second revised edition, New York: Crossroads.

Gallucci, C., Van Lare, M., Yoon, I., and Boatright, B. (2010) Instructional coaching: Building theory about the role and organizational support for professional learning, *American Educational Research Journal*, 47(4): 919–963.

Gergen, M. M. and Gergen, K. J. (2000) Qualitative inquiry: Tensions and transformations, in N. K. Denzin and Y. S. Lincoln (eds.) *Handbook of Qualitative Research*, second edition, Beverly Hills, CA: Sage, pp. 1025–1046.

Glaser, B. and Strauss, A. (1967) *The Discovery of Grounded Theory*, New York: Aldine.

Guba, E. G. (1990) Subjectivity and objectivity, in E. Eisner and A. Peshkin (eds.), *Qualitative Research in Education: The continuing debate*, New York: Teachers College Press, pp. 74–91.

Habermas, J. (1971) *Knowledge and Human Interest*, trans. J. J. Shapiro, Boston, MA: Beacon Press.

Halling, S. and Lawrence, C. (1999) Social constructionism: Homogenizing the world, negating embodied experience, *Journal of Theoretical and Philosophical Psychology*, 19(1): 78–89.

Harré, R. (1986) An outline of the social constructionist viewpoint, in R. Harré (ed.), *The Social Construction of Emotion*, Oxford: Basil Blackwell, pp. 2–14.

Harré, R. (1989) Metaphysics and methodology: some prescriptions for social psychology research, *European Journal of Social Psychology*, 19(5): 439–453.

Harré, R. and Tissaw, M. (2005) *Wittgenstein and Psychology: A practical guide*, Aldershot: Ashgate Publishing.

Harré, R. and van Langenhove, L. (eds.) (1999) *Positioning Theory: Moral contexts of intentional action*, Malden, MA: Blackwell.

Heidegger, M. (1962 [1923]) *Being and Time*, trans. J. Macquarrie and E. Robinson, New York: Harper & Row.

Held, B. (1998) The many truths of postmodernist discourse, *Journal of Theoretical and Philosophical Psychology*, 18(2): 193–217.

Henwood, K. and Pidgeon, N. (2003) Grounded theory in psychological research, in P. M. Camic, J. E. Rhodes, and L. Yarley (eds.) *Qualitative Research in Psychology: Expanding perspectives in methodology*, Washington, DC: American Psychological Association.

Hesse-Biber, S. N. (2010) *Mixed Methods Research: Merging theory with practice*, London: Guilford.

Hinde, R. A. (1997) *Relationships: A dialectical perspective*, Hove: Psychology Press.

Holmqvist, M., Gustavsson, L., and Wernberg, A. (2007) Generative learning: Learning beyond the learning situation, *Educational Action Research*, 15(2): 181–208.

Howe, K. R. (2009) Epistemology, methodology, and education science: Positivist dogmas, rhetoric, and the education science question, *Educational Researcher*, 38(6): 428–440.

Hunt, M. (1993) *The Story of Psychology*, London: Doubleday.

Joas, H. (1997) *G. H. Mead: A contemporary re-examination of his thought*, Cambridge, MA: MIT Press.

Johnson, G. M., Staton, A. Q., and Jorgensen-Earp, C. R. (1995) An ecological perspective on the transition of new university students, *Communication Education*, 44(4): 336–352.

Johnson, R. B. (2009) Comments on Howe: Toward a more inclusive "Scientific research in education", *Educational Researcher*, 38(6): 449–457.

Kretzmann, J. P., McKnight, J. L., Dobrowolski, S., and Puntenney, D. (2005) *Discovering Community Power: A guide to mobilizing local assets and your organization's capacity*, Asset-Based Community Development Institute School of Education and Social Policy, online, available at: www.abcdinstitute.org/docs/kelloggabcd.pdf (retrieved August 1, 2010).

Kuhn, D. (1995) Microgenetic study of change: What has it told us? *Psychological Science*, 6(3): 133–139.

Kuhn, D. (2005) *Thinking in Education*, Cambridge: Harvard University Press.

Lease, A. M., McFall, R. M., and Viken, R. J. (2003) Distance from peers in the group's perceived organizational structure: Relationships to individual characteristics, *Journal of Early Adolescence*, 23(2): 194–217.

Lincoln, Y. S. and Guba, E. G. (1985) *Naturalistic Inquiry*, Beverly Hills, CA: Sage.

Lincoln, Y. S. and Guba, E. G. (2000) Pragmatic controversies, contradictions, and emerging confluences, in N. K. Denzin and Y. S. Lincoln (eds.) *Handbook of Quantitative Research*, second edition, Thousand Oaks, CA: Sage, pp. 163–188.

Lovett, S. B. and Pillow, B. H. (2010) Age-related changes in children's and adults' explanations of interpersonal actions, *The Journal of Genetic Psychology*, 171(2): 139–167.

Lussier, R. N. (2010) *Publish Don't Perish: 100 tips that improve your ability to get published*, Charlotte, NC: Information Age Publishing, Inc.

Marton, F. (1986) Phenomenography: A research approach investigating different understandings of reality, *Journal of Thought*, 21(2): 28–49.

Marton, F. and Säljö, R. (1976) On qualitative differences in learning. I. Outcome and process, *British Journal of Educational Psychology*, 46(1): 4–11.

Marton, F. and Säljö, R. (1997) Approaches to learning, in F. Marton, D. Hounsell, and N. Entwistle (eds.) *The Experience of Learning, Implications for Teaching and Studying in Higher Education*, Edinburgh: Scottish Academic Press.

Maykut, P. and Morehouse, R. (1994) *Beginning Qualitative Research: A philosophical and practical guide*, London: Routledge.

McAdams, D. P. and Pals, J. L. (2006) A new big five: Fundamental principles for an integrative science of personality, *American Psychologist*, 61(3): 204–217.

McGrath, J. E. and Johnson, B. A. (2003) Methodology makes meaning: Qualitative and quantitative paradigms shape evidence and its interpretation, in P. M. Camic, J. E. Rhodes, and L. Yardley (eds). *Qualitative Research in Psychology: Expanding perspectives in methodology and design*, Washington, DC: American Psychological Association.

Mead, G. H. (1903) The definition of the psychical, *Decennial Publication of the University of Chicago*, first series, 3: 77–112.

Mead, G. H. (1913) The social self, *Journal of Philosophical, Psychological and Scientific Methods*, 10(14): 374–380.

Merleau-Ponty, M. (1962) *Phenomenology of Perception*, trans. C. Smith, London: Routledge & Kegan Paul.

Morehouse, R. (2000) The nature of academic disciplines: Philip Phenix's model applied to person, college and community, in D. Murray (ed.) *Person, College, and Community*, La Crosse, WI: Viterbo University.

Morehouse, R., Sakharuk, A and Kadieva, V. D. (2007) *Self-theories of Intelligence for University Tutors and Tutees*, poster at American Psychological Association annual meeting.

Morehouse, R. E. and Early, S. M. (2008). *Lab Observation Matrix*, La Crosse, WI: Viterbo University unpublished document.

Morehouse, R. E., Sakharuk, A., Merry, S., Kadieva, V., and Nesberg, M. (2009) A microgenetic study of the tutoring process: Learning centre research, *Journal of Pedagogical Research and Scholarship*, 1(2): 13–25.

Moya, C. J. (1990) *The Philosophy of Action: An introduction*, Cambridge: Polity Press.

Murray, M. (2003) Narrative psychology, in P. M. Camic, J. E. Rhodes, and L. Yarley (eds.) *Qualitative Research in Psychology: Expanding perspectives in methodology*, Washington, DC: American Psychological Association.

Oláh, L. N., Lawrence, N. R., and Riggan, M. (2003) Learning to learn from benchmark assessment data: How teachers analyze results, *Peabody Journal of Education*, 85(2): 226–245.

Patton, M. Q. (1990) *Qualitative Evaluation and Research Methods*, second edition, Newbury, CA: Sage.

Perkins, D. N. (1995) *Outsmarting IQ: The emerging science of learnable intelligence*, New York: Free Press.

Perkins, D. N. (1996) *Knowledge as Design*, Hillsdale, NJ: Lawrence Erlbaum Associates.

Phenix, P. (1970) The use of disciplines as curriculum content, in W. Becker and W. Dumas (eds.), *American Education: Foundation and superstructure*, Scranton, PA: International Textbook.

Pillow, B. H., Lovett, S. B., and Hill, V. (2000) Children's, adolescents' and adults' reference to goals to explain interpersonal action, *Infant and Child Development*, 17(5): 471–489.

Potter, J. (2003) Discovery analysis and discursive psychology in P. M. Camic, J. E. Rhodes, and L. Yarley (eds.), *Qualitative Research in Psychology: Expanding perspectives in methodology*, Washington, DC: American Psychological Association.

Purdue Online Writing Lab (2010) online, available at: http://owl.english.purdue.edu/owl/resource/560/01 (retrieved January 14, 2011).

Ragoff, B. (2003) *The Cultural Nature of Human Development*, Oxford: Oxford University Press.

Rieber, R. W. and Robinson, D. K. (2001) *Wilhelm Wundt in history: The making of a scientific psychology*, New York: Kluwer Academic/Plenum Publisher.

Rosenthal, S. B. and Bourgeois, P. L. (1991) *Mead and Merleau-Ponty: Toward a common vision*, New York: State University of New York Press.

Ryan, R. M. and Deci, E. L. (2000) Self-determination theory and the facilitation of intrinsic motivation, social development, and well-being, *American Psychologist*, 55(1): 68–78.

Sammons, P., Day, C., Kington, A., Gu, Q., Stobart, G., and Smees, R. (2007) Exploring variations in teachers' work, lives and their effects on pupils: Key findings and implications from a longitudinal mixed-method study, *British Educational Research Journal*, 33(5): 681–701.

Schoenfeld, A. H. (2009) Design experiments, in J. Green, G. Camilli, and P. Elmore (eds.), *Handbook of Complementary Methods in Educational Research*, London: Routledge, pp. 193–205.

Sefton-Green, J., Thomson, P., Jones, K., and Bresler, L. (eds.) (2011) *Routledge International Handbook of Creative Learning*, London: Routledge.

Seligman, M. E. P. (1998) The president's address, *American Psychologist*, 54: 559–562.

Selman, R. J. (2003) *The Promotion of Social Awareness: Powerful lessons from the partnership of developmental theory and classroom practice*, New York: Russell Sage Foundation.

Siegel, H. (2009) Epistemological diversity and education research: Much ado about nothing much? *Educational Researcher*, 35(2): 3–12.

Siegler, R. (1996) *Emerging Minds: The process of change in children's thinking*, New York: Oxford University Press

Siegler, R. and Crowley, K. (1991) The microgenetic method: A direct means for studying cognitive development, *American Psychologist*, 46(6): 606–620.

Smith, L. (2009) Wittgenstein's rule-following paradox: How to resolve it with lessons from psychology, *New Ideas in Psychology*, 27(2): 228–242.

Spreckels, J. (2008) Identity negotiation in small stories among German adolescent girls, *Narrative Inquiry*, 18(1): 393–413.

Stake, R. E. (2006) *Multiple Case Study Analysis*, New York: Guilford.

Stake, R. E. (2010) *Qualitative Research: Studying how things work*, New York: Guilford.

Susswein, N. and Racine, T. P. (2009) Wittgenstein and not-just-in-the-head-cognition, *New Ideas in Psychology*, 27(2): 184–196.

Tait, H., Entwistle, N. J., and McCune, V. (1998) ASSIST: A reconceptualisation of the approaches to studying inventory, in C. Rust (ed.) *Improving Students as Learners*, Oxford: Oxford Brookes University, The Oxford Centre for Staff and Learning Development.

Talarico, J. M. (2009) Freshman flashbulbs: memories of unique and first-time events in stating college, *Psychology Press*, 17(3): 256–265.

Taylor, C. (1995) *Philosophical Arguments*, Cambridge, MA: Harvard University Press.

The Research Board Working Party on Ethical Practices in Psychological Research (2004) *Ethical Guidelines for the British Psychological Society: Guidelines for minimum standards of ethical approval in psychological research*, Leicester: British Psychological Society, p. 6, online, available at: www.bps.org.uk/downloadfile.cfm?file_uuid=2B522636-1143-DFD0-7E3D-E2B3AEFCACDE&ext=pdf (retrieved January 5, 2011).

Tillman, L. C. (2009) Comments on Howe: The never-ending educational science debate – I'm ready to move on, *Educational Researcher*, 38(6): 458–462.

Titchener, E. B. (1912) The schema of introspection, *American Journal of Psychology*, 23: 485–508, online, available at: http://psychclassics.yorku.ca/Titchener/introspection.htm.

Trout, J. D. (2008) Seduction without cause: Uncovering explanatory neurophilia, *Trends in Cognitive Science*, 12(8): 281–282.

Viterbo University (n.d.) Model Informed Consent form, online, available at: www.viterbo.edu/uploadedFiles/centers/ethics/irb/MODEL%20INFORMED%20CONSENT%20FORM.pdf.

Viterbo University (n.d.) Institutional Review Board (IRB), online, available at: www.viterbo.edu/irb (retrieved January 11, 2011).

Wang, M.-T. and Holcombe, R. (2010) Adolescents' perceptions of school environment, engagement, and academic achievement in middle school, *American Educational Research Journal*, 47(3): 633–662.

Westerman, M. A. (2004) Theory and research on practices, theory and research as practices: Hermeneutics and psychological inquiry, *Journal of Theoretical and Philosophical Psychology*, 24(2): 123–156.

Westerman, M. A. (2005) What is interpersonal behavior? A post-Cartesian approach to problematic interpersonal patterns and psychotherapy process, *Review of General Psychology*, 9(1): 16–34.

Westerman, M. A. (2006) Quantitative research as an interpretative enterprise: The mostly unacknowledged role of interpretation in research efforts and suggestions for explicitly interpretive quantitative investigations, *New Ideas in Psychology*, 24(3): 189–211.

Westerman, M. A. and Steen, E. M. (2007) Going beyond the internal-external dichotomy in clinical psychology: The theory of interpersonal defense as an example of a participatory model, *Theory and Psychology*, 17(2): 323–351.

Westerman, M. A. and Steen, E. M. (2009) Revisiting conflict and defense from an interpersonal perspective: Using structured role play to investigate the effects of conflict on defensive interpersonal behavior, *Psychoanalytic Psychology*, 26(4): 379–401.

Westerman, M. A., Eubanks-Carter, C., Ziebert, N. C., Jeffries, E. and Cosgrove, T. J. (2007) Methods for examining children's beliefs about the functional role played by defensive interpersonal behavior, *British Journal of Developmental Psychology*, 25(2): 293–311.

Winch, P. (1990 [1958]) *The Idea of Social Science and its Relation to Philosophy*, London: Routledge.

Yanchar, S. C. (2006) On the possibility of contextual-quantitative inquiry, *New Ideas in Psychology*, 24(3): 212–228.

Yanchar, S. C. and Williams, D. D. (2006) Reconsidering the compatibility thesis and eclecticism: Five proposed guidelines for method use, *Educational Researcher*, 35(9): 3–12.

Yudkin, B. (2006) *Critical Reading: Making sense of research papers in life sciences and medicine*, London: Routledge.

Index